The Napoleonic Wars: A Very Short Introduction

VERY SHORT INTRODUCTIONS are for anyone wanting a stimulating and accessible way in to a new subject. They are written by experts and have been translated into more than 40 different languages. The series began in 1995 and now covers a wide variety of topics in every discipline. The VSI library contains nearly 400 volumes—a Very Short Introduction to everything from Indian philosophy to psychology and American history—and continues to grow in every subject area.

Very Short Introductions available now:

ACCOUNTING Christopher Nobes
ADVERTISING Winston Fletcher
AFRICAN HISTORY John Parker and
    Richard Rathbone
AGNOSTICISM Robin Le Poidevin
ALEXANDER THE GREAT
    Hugh Bowden
AMERICAN HISTORY Paul S. Boyer
AMERICAN IMMIGRATION
    David A. Gerber
AMERICAN POLITICAL PARTIES
    AND ELECTIONS L. Sandy Maisel
AMERICAN POLITICS Richard M. Valelly
THE AMERICAN PRESIDENCY
    Charles O. Jones
ANAESTHESIA Aidan O'Donnell
ANARCHISM Colin Ward
ANCIENT EGYPT Ian Shaw
ANCIENT GREECE Paul Cartledge
THE ANCIENT NEAR EAST
    Amanda H. Podany
ANCIENT PHILOSOPHY Julia Annas
ANCIENT WARFARE Harry Sidebottom
ANGELS David Albert Jones
ANGLICANISM Mark Chapman
THE ANGLO-SAXON AGE John Blair
THE ANIMAL KINGDOM Peter Holland
ANIMAL RIGHTS David DeGrazia
THE ANTARCTIC Klaus Dodds
ANTISEMITISM Steven Beller
ANXIETY Daniel Freeman and
    Jason Freeman
THE APOCRYPHAL GOSPELS
    Paul Foster
ARCHAEOLOGY Paul Bahn

ARCHITECTURE Andrew Ballantyne
ARISTOCRACY William Doyle
ARISTOTLE Jonathan Barnes
ART HISTORY Dana Arnold
ART THEORY Cynthia Freeland
ASTROBIOLOGY David C. Catling
ATHEISM Julian Baggini
AUGUSTINE Henry Chadwick
AUSTRALIA Kenneth Morgan
AUTISM Uta Frith
THE AVANT GARDE David Cottington
THE AZTECS David Carrasco
BACTERIA Sebastian G. B. Amyes
BARTHES Jonathan Culler
THE BEATS David Sterritt
BEAUTY Roger Scruton
BESTSELLERS John Sutherland
THE BIBLE John Riches
BIBLICAL ARCHAEOLOGY Eric H. Cline
BIOGRAPHY Hermione Lee
THE BLUES Elijah Wald
THE BOOK OF MORMON Terryl Givens
BORDERS Alexander C. Diener and
    Joshua Hagen
THE BRAIN Michael O'Shea
THE BRITISH CONSTITUTION
    Martin Loughlin
THE BRITISH EMPIRE Ashley Jackson
BRITISH POLITICS Anthony Wright
BUDDHA Michael Carrithers
BUDDHISM Damien Keown
BUDDHIST ETHICS Damien Keown
CANCER Nicholas James
CAPITALISM James Fulcher
CATHOLICISM Gerald O'Collins

Mike Rapport

THE
NAPOLEONIC
WARS

A Very Short Introduction

OXFORD
UNIVERSITY PRESS

OXFORD
UNIVERSITY PRESS

Great Clarendon Street, Oxford, OX2 6DP,
United Kingdom

Oxford University Press is a department of the University of Oxford.
It furthers the University's objective of excellence in research, scholarship,
and education by publishing worldwide. Oxford is a registered trade mark of
Oxford University Press in the UK and in certain other countries

© Mike Rapport 2013

The moral rights of the author have been asserted

First Edition published in 2013
Impression: 5

British Library Cataloguing in Publication Data
Data available

ISBN 978-0-19-959096-4

Printed in Great Britain by
Ashford Colour Press Ltd, Gosport, Hampshire

For Helen, with love and gratitude, as always,
and for Nico: Semper Fi!

Contents

List of illustrations

Introduction

The French Revolutionary and Napoleonic Wars of 1792–1815 were amongst the longest and the most intense conflicts ever experienced in Europe: for a similar scale of destruction and brutality, one would have to look back to the Thirty Years War of 1618–48 and to the world wars of the twentieth century. The Napoleonic Wars of 1803–15 alone destroyed five million lives, which matches the eight to ten million slaughtered during the First World War, if the overall size of the European population is taken into account. The French Revolutionary Wars of 1792–1802 wasted a further two million lives. The intensity of the violence was such that *one fifth* of the 3,372 European battles fought between *c.*1490 and 1815 occurred between 1792 and 1815. The conflicts were also global in their reach: although not habitually given the name 'world war', they had truly worldwide repercussions which made a lasting mark across the earth.

The figure who casts his distinctive shadow across this period is Napoleon Bonaparte, adored and demonized both then and since in equal measure. His meteoric rise from minor nobility in Corsica, where he was born in 1769, to become the single most powerful ruler in Europe would not have been possible without the French Revolution of 1789. Trained at the military academy at Brienne, then at the École Militaire in Paris, he took a commission

1

in the artillery in 1785. From his Corsican background Napoleon carried a clannishness that led him to advance the interests of his family throughout his career—but only for so long as they served his own political power: while Napoleon could justly be accused of nepotism, his aspirations were not dynastic, but rather he aimed at satisfying his drive for power. He therefore removed family members from office when they challenged him or failed to meet his expectations. As a young man, he absorbed the classics, identifying strongly with Alexander the Great, as well as the enlightened ideas of the age, including eighteenth-century notions of patriotism and political reform. Bonaparte was also a seething knot of resentment and frustration, nourishing an impulse for violence which verged on the sadistic. He was an 'outsider' without connections in French society, disadvantages which drove him harder. His violent outbursts may have stemmed from his brutal upbringing by domineering parents and from a bitter competitiveness with his siblings. He could be charming in his relationships with individuals, but he brooked no opposition to his desires and ambitions, a characteristic that he later transferred into politics and diplomacy. Bonaparte was a master propagandist: as a general in the French revolutionary armies, he deftly crafted an image of himself as a military hero and genius. He was, above all, an opportunist (see Figure 1).

Historians have debated Napoleon's policies during the wars: was he trying to integrate Europe, unifying it by reforming its social and political structures? Or was the Napoleonic Empire simply a system of conquest aimed only at the exploitation of Europe's people and resources? The historian Paul Schroeder argues that there was an ideological vacuum at the heart of Napoleon's domination of Europe: it was a criminal enterprise seeking power for its own sake, matched only by the Nazis: 'Hitler did it for the sake of an unbelievably horrible ideal; Napoleon for no underlying purpose at all.' The central problem in this interpretation was Napoleon himself: no matter how hard the other European powers tried to accommodate him, Napoleon simply did not—could not—accept

2

1. David's painting shows that the heroic myth of Napoleon was already well formed by 1800. In reality, the First Consul crossed the mountains on a mule

limits to his power, which explains why he was never able to stabilize his European empire and why the wars continued until its final destruction. While far from absolving Napoleon of blame, this book will seek to nuance such views.

The very scale of Napoleon's ambitions, it has been argued, distinguished the Napoleonic Wars from their eighteenth-century precursors. As the historian Charles Esdaile has argued, even the leaders of the French Revolution set strategic limits to their expansionism. This is true, but just as Napoleon was a creature of the French Revolution, so the Napoleonic Wars of 1803–15 were rooted in the French Revolutionary Wars of 1792–1802. A ten-month peace separated the two conflicts and they shared many of the same causes and issues, so it is natural that historians should treat them as one, great overarching conflagration, the 'French Wars'. The continuity across the period is given explicit recognition by the fact that, although there were in fact not two but seven separate wars, they are customarily counted by the successive alliances formed against the French, from the First Coalition in 1792 to the Seventh that finally destroyed Napoleon's ambitions in 1815. Collectively, the wars spilled out across Europe, from Ireland to Russia and from Scandinavia to the Balkans, but, in their imperial reach, they also meshed with conflicts across the world, in the Middle East, India and South-East Asia, at points along the African coast, and in the Americas.

This book acknowledges some stark differences between the French Revolutionary and Napoleonic Wars, but it treats the 'French Wars' as a whole, since a full understanding of one is difficult without an awareness of the other. While accepting that aggressive French expansionism, whether French Revolutionary or Napoleonic, was the single most important reason for the agonizingly long protraction of the carnage, it argues that it is not the full explanation. The entire series of conflicts had causes that went far beyond any single factor, and which were beyond the control of any one ruler. Rather, it is argued here that, as French power surged across Europe from 1792, it worked on long-term tensions in international politics which also reached boiling point. The wars, in other words, were not just about French expansionism or Napoleon's ambition, but represented a perfect storm in which a range of European crises came together.

One of the reasons the wars lasted for so long and the French were so hard to defeat was that France's opponents could not or would not focus all their military efforts on victory over the French: they were either distracted by other crises, or bent on exploiting the international meltdown in the pursuit of their own, habitual strategic goals. It follows from this that the French Wars were not an ideological conflict between the French Revolution and Napoleon on the one hand and the old regime powers of Europe on the other, but originated in the deep, structural problems in eighteenth-century international politics, while the belligerents were motivated primarily by such objectives as dynastic expansion and strategic security. The first three chapters seek to demonstrate all this, Chapter 1 by exploring the causes of the wars and Chapters 2 and 3 by narrating the course of the conflict between 1792 and 1815. Yet the denial of ideology as a primary cause of the conflict and its painful prolongation does not mean that it was unimportant in other ways. The warring nations mobilized their peoples with powerful rhetorical, symbolic, and material appeals to their loyalty, their commitment to the social and political order, and their religious beliefs. So if the French Wars were not truly ideological in their origins (although surely the inflammatory rhetoric on both sides did not help soothe matters), they did become ideological in the ways in which states tried to motivate their people. Chapters 4 and 7 explore these issues of ideology and reform: how the structures of the French revolutionary state managed to fuel France's war effort and how its opponents responded through reform and seeking ways of mobilizing their own publics in defence of the old order. These chapters sandwich in two others, 5 and 6, which describe the experience of war at the 'sharp end', for soldiers, sailors, and civilians: these views from the front line and at the grassroots act as a counter-balance to the first three chapters, which look at the wars very much from a strategic and diplomatic perspective. The book concludes by discussing the long-term impact of the war to show that we are still living with its legacy today.

Chapter 1
Origins

> The whole plain, which had looked so lovely and bright
> earlier in the day with all those puffs of smoke and the
> bayonets glinting in the morning sunshine, was now
> shrouded in a cloud of dark, damp mist and smoke reeking
> with the strange, pungent smell of saltpetre and blood.
> One or two dark clouds had come up, and a fine drizzle
> was sprinkling the dead, the wounded, the fearful, the
> weary and the wavering. 'Good people, that's enough,' it
> seemed to say. 'Stop and think. What are you doing?'

The French Revolutionary and Napoleonic Wars seared
themselves on the nineteenth-century consciousness: Leo Tolstoy's
vivid evocation of the battlefield of Borodino—a brutal clash of
arms west of Moscow on 7 September 1812, between the Russians
and Napoleon's *Grande Armée*—presents a vision of hell which
compels nature itself to appeal against human barbarity. Other
writers remembered the conflicts of 1792–1815 as the 'Great War'
until the phrase was applied to the industrialized slaughter of
millions on the killing fields of Europe during the First World War
and, like that cataclysm, the French Wars represented the collapse
of the existing international order. They were indeed a struggle
of catastrophic proportions: this chapter explains why such a
conflict arose towards the end of the eighteenth century.

The European international system

The French Revolutionary and Napoleonic Wars erupted from a series of chronic spasms that had racked the international order of eighteenth-century Europe. International relations were structured around five great powers, which had conflicting strategic aspirations: Britain, France, the German kingdom of Prussia, Austria (which held sway over a vast multinational empire in Central and Eastern Europe), and Russia. The British tried to shy away from continental embroilments, since they distracted from their money-spinning in trade and empire, activities that they were coming to dominate globally. Yet they could not escape the need to assure the security of their home waters in Europe, since they had lethal rivals jealous of their commercial and imperial success.

Chief among these was France: the two powers had regularly clashed in India and North America and, while the British had the whip hand after their triumph in the Seven Years War (1756–63), the French had their revenge by helping Britain's rebellious American colonists, who were also allied to the Dutch and the Spanish, win their freedom in the American War of Independence (1775–83). Yet the French could never land a decisive blow against British imperial dominance, partly because they were caught in a strategic cleft stick. France's eighteenth-century Bourbon monarchs aspired to imperial, maritime glory, but the geopolitical reality was that the kingdom was also a continental power. Its greatest vulnerability was along its northern frontier, where the French confronted their other mortal rivals, the Austrians. Austria's venerable ruling dynasty, the Habsburgs, ruled most of modern-day Belgium (the Austrian Netherlands) and the Austrian Emperor exercised indirect authority in Germany, frustrating French territorial expansion north and eastwards towards a secure, defensible frontier, the most ambitious of which was the River Rhine. This French pressure—and resistance to it—littered the Low Countries and the Rhineland with battlefields, turning the region into the 'cock-pit of Europe'.

Austrian influence in Germany arose from the fact that, with very rare exceptions in the past, the Habsburg Emperor was also Holy Roman Emperor. The Holy Roman Empire was a loose Central European confederation of 365 primarily German states—kingdoms, principalities, bishoprics, cities, and lordships—that corresponded with modern Germany, Austria, Slovenia, the Czech Republic, and a little beyond. Some of the rulers in the Empire were Electors, with the right to choose the Holy Roman Emperor on the death of his predecessor. It was logical that Austria's Habsburgs should be the perennial choice: as rulers of the most powerful military state in the region, they were able to protect what was otherwise Europe's 'soft centre' from foreign assault.

Yet over the course of the eighteenth century, Austria's position in the Empire was threatened by Prussia to the north. With its formidable army and aggressive absolute monarchs, Prussia had gradually grown at the expense of its neighbours since the end of the Thirty Years War in 1648 and became Austria's great challenger for German hegemony. Aspiring to bind together its scattered territories into one great, contiguous kingdom, by 1792 Prussia made up 19 per cent of all the Empire's territory, but its eastward expansion, engulfing Polish territory from 1772, was more dramatic still. Austria sought to shore up its position against Prussia to the north, but its ruling monarchs also ruled a dynastic empire, which overlapped with the Holy Roman Empire and encompassed a polyglot, multi-ethnic sweep of peoples across Central and Eastern Europe: Austrians, Czechs, Slovaks, Hungarians, Italians, Slovenians, Croats, Serbs, Romanians, Poles, and Ukrainians. While Habsburg territory in Italy made the Austrians the single most important power in the peninsula, the expanse of Austria's empire in Eastern Europe had brought it into frequent conflict with the Ottoman Empire (or Turkey, whose Sultan ruled the Balkans) and, increasingly over the course of the eighteenth century, on collision course with the emerging might of Russia. Austria's overriding goal may have been to expand into the

Balkans at the expense of Turkey, but it also had to ensure its security against the trio of real or potential threats: from France, from Prussia, and from Russia.

Russia's emergence in the eighteenth century under the autocratic tsars and tsarinas was a dramatic story, one which began under Tsar Peter the Great (1682–1725), who rebranded his kingdom as the 'Russian Empire', a change from the traditional 'Muscovy'. Westward expansion came at the expense of the once-great powers of the Baltic and Eastern Europe—Sweden, Poland, and the Ottoman Empire. Yet Russia also incurred new strategic anxieties, namely the security of its western frontiers against such real and potential threats as Austria and Prussia. Moreover, Russia's concerns were not only European, but Eurasian. Its expansion, southwards into the Black Sea region, the Caucasus, Central Asia, and eastwards into Siberia and Alaska, was particularly breathtaking under Catherine the Great (1762–96), but it brought Russia into conflict with Turkey and Persia, with the nomadic tribes along the undefined Asian borderlands, occasional friction with the Chinese Empire, and, potentially, put it on collision course with the British in South Asia. For some Russian strategists by 1800, the British imperial presence there posed the single greatest long-term obstacle to Russian expansion in Eurasia and the Pacific. The British were beginning to reciprocate, seeing in Russia a distant but ever-looming strategic threat.

In struggling to meet their ambitions, the great powers buffeted, squeezed, and sometimes shattered a range of 'secondary' powers such as the United Provinces (the Netherlands), Portugal, Spain, the two Italian kingdoms of Piedmont-Sardinia and Naples, Sweden, Poland, and the Ottoman Empire. While these states were either in decline from their sixteenth- or seventeenth-century heydays, or had never seriously aspired to European greatness, they were all of some account in military or commercial terms: the Dutch, Portuguese, and Spanish still held substantial maritime empires and the navies to defend them, while the Poles, the Swedes, the Turks, the Piedmontese, and the Neapolitans fielded armies and, in most cases, floated navies, that could give the great powers pause, especially when they acted with allies. Every one of these states would be engulfed along with the great powers in the conflict that consumed Europe after 1792.

All international systems are afflicted with tensions and rivalries; all states are periodically tempted to use violence to achieve their ends. Yet the question arises as to why Europe's international politics at the end of the eighteenth century proved to be especially combustible. Part of the answer lies in the conduct of international relations, which were driven by the concern with what diplomats called the 'balance of power'. This was based on the assumption that in pursuing their own interests, states and rulers ultimately achieved stability in the international order and a minimum guarantee of security for individual states—or at least for the stronger ones. A ruler was therefore justified in being motivated by *raison d'état*, meaning the aggressive pursuit of the interests of his or her state—its power, wealth, and security—as well as the prestige, honour, and rank of the dynasty. Moreover, it was assumed that the essential relationship was that between the prince and his territory, not between the ruler and a people of a given nationality: this was a Europe where sovereigns still regarded the countries they ruled as their inheritance, leaving little room for such concepts as national self-determination. When one kingdom became considerably stronger than the others, threatening hegemony over the continent, then the general interest of all other states was to coalesce and to cut their over-mighty rival down to size, so restoring the balance of power.

One corollary of this process was an obsession with 'compensations': if one power gained in territory or wealth through war, treaty, or dynastic marriage, then its rivals claimed the right to acquisitions roughly equivalent in value. Also essential were alliances, which were not aimed at maintaining a permanent, stable order, but rather at furthering the aims of the individual allies, which was why such alignments could be quite suddenly reversed. The 'balance of power', therefore, rationalized a brutally competitive international states system, in which the essential dynamic was the pursuit of individual, dynastic interest. Moreover, in a pre-industrial world, before rapid economic development provided states with a sustained expansion in domestic wealth, the quickest and most effective way of securing the resources upon which military power was based—above all, population and taxable wealth—was through territorial conquest, which also had the benefit of denying one's rivals the same.

In this environment, there were no fewer than sixteen wars fought between two or more of the major European powers between 1700 and 1790. The price of failure was, at best, amputation (Austria lost its rich province of Silesia to Prussia in 1740), at worst, utter evisceration: Poland disappeared as an independent state altogether in three successive partitions of its territory in 1772, 1793, and 1795. The more enlightened rulers of eighteenth-century Europe were certainly alive to humanitarian motives as they rejuvenated their legal systems, encouraged economic growth, and reduced the power of the Church and nobility. Yet their reforms were fundamentally driven by an urgent need to keep afloat in turbulent international waters, boosting the state's ability to wage war by ensuring that their subjects were prosperous and loyal and the administration efficient in taxing and recruiting them. Symptomatic of the unforgiving nature of European diplomatic relations was the way in which four long-term, smouldering problems fused into the final meltdown of the eighteenth-century political system, the French Wars of 1792–1815.

These issues were France's dual concern for continental security and global power; the emergence of Russia; the rivalry between Prussia and Austria in Germany; and the friction between Europe's maritime empires, particularly France and Britain.

Together, these factors created the poisonous conditions from which reared the French Revolutionary and Napoleonic Wars. They also ensured that the European conflicts of 1792–1815 would have repercussions around the world.

For most of the eighteenth century, France under the Bourbon monarchy was continental Europe's greatest power: populous and enjoying reserves of real economic wealth. Yet in pursuing its strategic security on the European continent, France struggled to meet its other ambition: to challenge the British for dominance of global trade, imperial hegemony, and the riches that these offered to sustain French prestige and power. This 'amphibious' policy—both continental and maritime—put intense financial and political strain on the state: France's armed forces were bled white and the royal treasury dangerously drained during the bitter humiliation of the Seven Years War and the successful but costly intervention in the American War of Independence. The kingdom's disastrous financial deficit, combined with its stand-off against the elites who obstructed its efforts at reform and a hostile public which did not trust the motives of 'despotic' royal ministries, brought about the collapse of the absolute monarchy in the French Revolution of 1789. It also left patriotic French citizens with a burning sense of wounded pride. Even the widely read political philosopher the Abbé Guillaume Raynal, renowned for his courageous attack on slavery and imperialism, complained of France's fall from global predominance:

> The French Navy, which had been once—just once—so redoubtable, had ceased to exist. Weakness, disorder and corruption have reduced it once more to the oblivion from which it had emerged during the brightest epoch of the Monarchy. It could no longer defend our most far-flung possessions, nor protect our coasts from invasion and pillage. On every shore of the globe, our navigators, our merchants, were exposed to ruinous snubs and humiliations a hundred times more intolerable.

Yet within a few years, the construction of a 'new France' by the French Revolution unleashed a resurgence of French power which was one of the primary forces driving the great wars of 1792–1815.

The crisis of French power also arose because its rivals were becoming more muscular: overseas, that meant Britain, but on the continent, it was, above all, Russia. Ever since the days when Peter the Great broke Swedish power in northern Europe, Russia had been making its presence felt in European politics. Two other powers lay in the path of this slow but relentless juggernaut: Poland and the Ottoman Empire. Since Poland and Turkey were traditional French allies, their successive collisions with Russia also contributed to the crumpling of France's influence in Eastern Europe. In 1772, Poland had territory hacked off by the predatory powers of Russia, Austria, and Prussia in the first of the three eighteenth-century partitions. While Russia advanced into Europe, it also pushed southwards, against the Ottoman Empire, and it was the aggressive expansionism under Catherine the Great that jolted the other European powers into taking notice, as the balance of power in the Black Sea and the Balkans definitively shifted towards Russia, which supplanted Austria as Turkey's mortal enemy in the region. In 1776, the *Scots Magazine* remarked that 'Russia enjoys her power, influence, and glory, with a noble and splendid magnificence...She sits supreme between Europe and Asia, and looks as if she intended to dictate to both.' The question of Russian expansion was one of the great issues at stake in the Napoleonic Wars.

Until its political erasure in 1795, Poland had cushioned the Holy Roman Empire from Russia's westward thrusts, but Germany was itself a battleground as Austria was challenged by the northern upstart, Prussia. The gauntlet was thrown down by Frederick the Great (1740–86), who soon after his accession struck at the Austrians, and in the 'rape of Silesia', wrested one of the richest provinces from the Habsburgs' grasp. It was the start of a long and bitter struggle for German hegemony which would not be resolved until Bismarck secured Prussia's victory in 1866: Frederick himself wrote in 1752 that 'never will [Austria] forget that it must now share its authority in Germany with us'. For Europe, the significance of the Austro-Prussian rivalry was that it was a further cause of international instability. It provoked a mind-boggling diplomatic reversal at the start of the Seven Years War: an alliance between those other bitter enemies, Austria and France, in 1756. The former hoped to harness French military muscle to reconquer Silesia, while the French hoped that Austria would pursue the war in Europe, leaving them free to rake their fire against the British overseas.

It did not turn out that way: France was humbled by the Prussians in Europe and by the British in India and Canada. French public anger was vented not against Prussia (Frederick was admired as an enlightened ruler), but against the Austrians, since it was widely believed that they had given little in return for French sacrifices. The future Louis XVI's Austrian bride, Marie-Antoinette, would be a target of this Austrophobic venom after the couple married in 1770. One of the causes of the French Wars in 1792 was this visceral French distrust of Austria, but public opinion reserved a special place of torment for France's greatest enemy, Britain.

Maritime rivalries such as those between Britain and France gave the French Revolutionary and Napoleonic Wars their global dimension: Europe's eighteenth-century wars were fought overseas as well as on the continent. In the mercantilist thinking of the age, empires and control of trade were essential to the might of the naval powers of Western Europe, such as Britain, France, Spain, Portugal, and the Netherlands. The world's wealth was finite, the logic ran, so the challenge for competing states was for each to try to capture as much of it as possible and to deny their rivals the same. This lay beneath the European imperial systems which sought to exclude foreigners from their colonial trade in such commodities as spices, tea, cotton, silk, gold and silver, coffee, sugar, and indigo—the last three of which were produced by the toil, tears, sweat, and the blood of slaves. The money creamed off from imperial commerce and, sometimes, from direct taxation on the colonies gave governments the finances, and, more importantly, the credit on Europe's financial markets, to bankroll their considerable military expenses. Imperial rivalries were therefore among the most sensitive sources of conflict between the European powers, as their colonists, their merchants, and their navies pressed, probed, and collided with each other. Fighting often started in the colonies even before war was declared in Europe and, once that happened, the European empires in the Americas and Asia were the scenes of some major battles.

The most bitter of all these imperial contests arose between the British and the French. This was not just because of the geographical proximity of the two powers in Europe, but also because both had sought to exploit the decline of the early starters in European overseas expansion, namely the Portuguese, the Spanish, and the Dutch. During the eighteenth century, the French and the British had emerged as the predominant imperial powers. While Britain always held the lead, France made great strides: the value of French overseas commerce more than tripled between 1716 and 1787 and within that figure, its colonial trade—mostly with its islands in the Caribbean—increased tenfold, an acceleration that continued right up to the outbreak of war with Britain in 1793. For all their commercial energy, however, the French were never able to mount a successful military challenge to the British, except for when they combined their naval forces with allies among the other maritime powers. The combination of French, Dutch, and Spanish naval forces during the American War of Independence explains why, for a crucial moment in 1781, the overstretched British lost their maritime dominance, allowing a Franco-American army to land the decisive blow at Yorktown. During the French Wars of 1792–1815, French alliances with Spain and their dominance of the Netherlands would be critical to their struggle against Britain.

Imperialism also ensured that the conflict had truly global repercussions. A memorandum from the leading French citizens of Pondichéry, one of France's few remaining Indian colonies, warned in 1790 that 'a lasting peace between France and Britain is a beautiful chimera invented by a love of humanity'.

The crisis of the international order, 1787–1792

All these long-term challenges fused together catastrophically in the French Revolutionary and Napoleonic Wars. The conflict was the result of a protracted and complex crisis in European politics between 1787 and 1792, of which the French Revolution was a part. The three forces driving Europe towards disaster were another surge of Russian power in the east, the Revolution in France, and one of those startling diplomatic reversals characteristic of the age: an alliance between Austria and Prussia. Russian expansion, as before, came at the expense of Turkey and Poland. The international ramifications of the Russo-Turkish War that broke out in August 1787 were complex, but for now the essential point is that by the time peace was made in January 1792, the Russian position on the Black Sea was even stronger than before. The next victim was Poland, where King Stanisław August Poniatowski, Catherine the Great's onetime lover, refused to be the Tsarina's performing poodle and embarked on a series of reforms aimed at strengthening the Polish state. Taking advantage of Russian embroilment in the Turkish war, the King and the parliament (*sejm*) produced Europe's first written constitution on 3 May 1791, posing a direct challenge to Russia. A reinvigorated Poland, particularly in alliance with the Ottoman Empire, might check Russia's expansion. Faced with an irate Tsarina, who publicly claimed that Poland was infected with revolutionary 'Jacobinism', Stanisław knew that his kingdom could only survive with allies, but Poland's traditional friend, France, was in no state to assist. The Russians invaded in May 1792, just as the French Revolutionary Wars erupted in the west. Russia and Prussia stripped away more territory from Poland in the Second Partition of 1793, but worse was to come. The 'Polish question' continued to fester and would flare up at critical moments in the coming European conflict.

In the west, France in 1789—to the frankly gleeful relief of many Europeans—looked to be out of action for a long time. That its near-bankruptcy had sapped its military energy had already been rudely exposed in 1787, when the Prussians, supported by the British, crushed a revolution in the Netherlands which had established a democratic, pro-French regime. The French could only gnash their teeth: 'This act of weakness and the triumph of our enemies astounded me', wrote the French diplomat Louis-Philippe de Ségur. 'From that moment I saw the abyss yawning, into which feeble government on one side and unbridled passions on the other were dragging my fatherland and its king.' When the absolute monarchy collapsed in 1789, the revolutionaries, well aware of France's enfeeblement, worked hard to avoid international confrontation. On 22 May 1790, when war against Britain seemed possible because of a naval incident on the Nootka Sound off the west coast of Canada, the French National Assembly renounced all wars of conquest: 'the French nation...will never employ her strength against the liberty of any people.' Yet some events could not help but cause tensions. Right from the start, conservative nobles, army officers, and clergymen fled the Revolution and gathered in some of the German principalities. These *émigrés* started to gather an army under the Prince de Condé, who noisily demanded Austrian intervention to restore the old order in France. Emperor Leopold II of Austria saw them for what they were, a shrill though ineffective bunch of troublemakers, but the presence of an *émigré* army understandably inflamed French fears of invasion. There were other tensions, such as demands for compensation from the German princes who had lands in Alsace, but who had lost their sovereign rights when the National Assembly abolished what it called 'feudalism' in August 1789 and, in September 1791, the French annexation of the Papal enclaves of Avignon and the Comtat Venaissin. These issues were not enough to spark war: in neither case did any great

17

European power stir, but the two incidents were clear messages from the Revolution: France would be guided not by old regime treaties, but by the principle of national self-determination.

What drove France towards conflict were the internal dynamics of revolutionary politics. Part of the problem was King Louis XVI's deep reluctance to rule as a constitutional monarch. In the fateful 'Flight to Varennes' in June 1791, he tried to flee the country with his family, provoking a political crisis in Paris: how could a constitutional monarchy function when its crowned head had unambiguously shown that he wanted no part in it? A republican movement was already stirring as Louis made his humiliating return to the capital, but enough moderates remained who wanted the new constitution to work. Republicanism was violently suppressed in July and the King accepted the Constitution of 1791 in September. Yet the elections to the new Legislative Assembly returned a powerful left-wing phalanx of deputies, soon called the Girondins, since many of their most lucid orators came from the south-western Gironde region. Convinced that Louis's acceptance of the constitution was bogus, they sought to expose it as such and to take power in the process. The Girondins believed that war against the princes of the Holy Roman Empire who sheltered the *émigrés* (which also meant war against Austria, since Leopold was Emperor) would force the King to declare himself, between France and its enemies, between revolution and counter-revolution.

Meanwhile, a group on the right, the 'Fayettists', calculated that a conflict would force the King to rely on the hero of the American war Lafayette for victory, after which the general would turn his sword against the fractious revolutionaries in Paris and bolster the power of the crown. In the centre were the monarchists, the Feuillants, who desired above all to make the constitution work and so opposed war. They had an unlikely ally in the left-winger Maximilien Robespierre, who was emerging as a leader of the Jacobins, another left-wing group with whom the

Girondins would soon acrimoniously split. He rebutted the arguments of the Girondins: 'no one loves armed missionaries,' he warned when one of their leaders, Jacques-Pierre Brissot, stirringly declared that the war would be a 'crusade for universal liberty'. Yet the Girondins won partly because Louis XVI himself secretly staked his future on the belief that in a war the Austrians would surely rout the French army, still recovering from the shock of revolution, and restore his authority. On 20 April 1792, therefore, the King asked the Legislative Assembly for a declaration of war. It was proclaimed with only seven dissenting votes. Europe would not know any long period of peace until 1815 (see Figure 2).

While the war in the west was certainly ignited by French domestic politics, it was also the result of a diplomatic realignment which dramatically, if temporarily, dampened one of the main sources of eighteenth-century conflict, the rivalry

Louis XVI a l'Assemblée législative avec ses ministres Jacoquins declarant la Guerre.

2. Louis XVI declares war on Austria as the deputies in the National Assembly cheer. They had conflicting motives for war and they helped unleash a conflict that engulfed Europe for more than twenty years

between Austria and Prussia. The *rapprochement* was an agonizing process, but it is here that the Russo-Turkish War of 1787–92 takes on special European significance. Austria, allied with Russia since 1781, had been dragged into the conflict against Turkey in 1788 and, as its army floundered in the Balkans and its Belgian, Hungarian, and Tyrolean subjects were either in revolt, or on the brink of it, Frederick William II of Prussia saw the opportunity to shatter the Habsburg Empire once and for all. Towards the end of 1789, Frederick William massed his army in Silesia, planning to strike at Austria in the spring. Fortunately for the Austrians, the tide turned in the Turkish war in the nick of time. In 1790, Emperor Leopold was able to disengage from the conflict, calm or crush the domestic opposition, and (in July) negotiate a peace agreement with the Prussians at Reichenbach.

Frederick William may have backed down, but he was frustrated: his invasion of the Netherlands in 1787 and his mobilization against Austria had brought no material gains for Prussia. He saw new opportunities at the expense of either a beleaguered Poland or a weakened France. As early as the autumn of 1790, he was suggesting to the Austrians that joint action against the latter might yield rich rewards. Leopold was not convinced until events in France took a radical turn after the Flight to Varennes in the summer of 1791. There followed a tragic blunder: in the Declaration of Pillnitz on 27 August, Frederick William and Leopold declared that the plight of Louis XVI was a matter of common concern to all sovereigns and that joint action was needed to restore his authority. While the Prussians were bent on territorial conquest, even now Leopold seems merely to have hoped that sabre-rattling would persuade the French to concentrate on stabilizing their domestic situation. He fatally miscalculated, because the revolutionaries in Paris took the declaration literally. It was from this moment that the inexorable slide to war began, for it was only as the war fever in Paris became more and more virulent that Leopold responded positively to Prussian proposals for a formal alliance for a military strike against France: it was signed on 7 February 1792. Although it was the French who actually declared war in April, the battle lines were already forming. So it was that, by the spring of 1792, two major crises were unfolding, one in the west, the other, concerning Poland, in the east. How and why these two conflicts fused into one single firestorm, engulfing all Europe, is a subject of the next chapter.

Chapter 2

The French Revolutionary Wars, 1792–1802

France blithely declared war against Austria in April 1792 because internal forces—the King, the Fayettists, and the Girondins—believed it was the way to political power. While individually they were working in very different directions, collectively they were united in one crucial sense: their calculations were horribly wrong. Louis XVI would be guillotined nine months into the conflict, Lafayette would desert to the enemy, and, while the Girondins certainly took power on the ruins of the constitutional monarchy in August 1792, they then struggled to master the crisis which they had helped to unleash. As France plunged into Terror, they were purged in June 1793 by their steelier Jacobin enemies—the more radical republicans, led by Robespierre, who pragmatically allied with the Paris crowd and argued for harsher measures to deal with the crisis—and their leaders were decapitated in a bloodbath in October. Rather than a quick and easy French victory, the war developed into a conflict which, by the end of the decade, would engulf all of Europe. This was because the struggle was less of an ideological conflict between the French Revolution and the old European order than a fusion of long-term international frictions. This is not to say that the French Revolution was irrelevant, since from this political crucible France emerged as the single most important, overriding challenge to European security (although contemporary statesmen did not always see it in these terms).

The war also chained the fate of the Revolution to its own unpredictable course: ultimately, it tortuously dragged the French Republic into the dictatorship of Napoleon Bonaparte. The Napoleonic Wars were not, however, in every sense a continuation of the French Revolutionary Wars. Aggressive and expansionist though the French Republic had been, Napoleon's ambitions were geographically even more expansive, aimed less at French strategic security than Napoleon's own ambitions for political power. Yet without both the French Revolution and the wars, Bonaparte would never have seized power in 1799 and he would never have inherited his single most important weapon: an invigorated France, awe-inspiring in its military might and its capacity for expansion. The aggressive expansionism of both the French Republic and Napoleon was certainly the single most important source of blame for prolonging the agony of the French Wars from 1792 to 1815. Yet it is not the only explanation: the other powers also aggressively and opportunistically pursued their own territorial and strategic interests even as French power surged across Europe. What that surge ultimately did was to fuse the depressingly diverse range of eighteenth-century international rivalries into a single, destructive firestorm. David Lloyd George's explanation for the First World War might equally apply to the French Wars: 'the nations...slithered over the brink into the boiling cauldron of war.'

The War of the First Coalition, 1792–1797

The French Revolutionary Wars are customarily defined as the struggles between France on the one hand and the First and Second Coalitions on the other, between 1792 and 1802. The First Coalition initially pitted Austria and Prussia, with the partial engagement of the Holy Roman Empire, against France in 1792, but by the spring of 1793, it had embraced Britain, the Netherlands, Spain, Piedmont-Sardinia, Naples, and Portugal. The coalition had fallen apart by October 1797 after one ally after another was either overrun by the French, or made a separate peace to secure the best possible terms, leaving only the British to fight on alone. Yet there was no respite for the continent, for in the summer of 1798 the war was reignited, the very geographic scale reflected in the membership of the Second Coalition, embroiling the Ottoman Empire and Russia alongside Britain, Austria, Portugal, and Naples. After its early victories, this alliance also broke apart. So exhausted were both sides that even France and Britain made peace in 1802 at Amiens, a treaty marking the end of the French Revolutionary Wars.

In the opening campaign in 1792, the calculations of the Austrians, that the French armies were a rabble, seemed to be borne out: the poorly trained volunteers broke and ran at the first encounter with the disciplined fire-power of the Austrians. As Prussia joined the war on 21 May, well might King Frederick William II's aide-de-camp, Johann von Bischoffwerder, have reassured some officers that 'the comedy will not last long. The army of lawyers will soon be crushed and we shall be back home by the autumn.' The Austro-Prussian armies began their slow but relentless advance into France in the summer, provoking the first major political crisis in the French Revolution linked to the war. The *sans-culottes*, the popular militants of Paris, rose up and, supported by National Guard units (the citizens' militia created in 1789), overthrew Louis XVI on 10 August 1792, a republic was proclaimed on 22 September 1792, and the King was guillotined on 21 January 1793. 'They threaten you with Kings!' thundered the great revolutionary orator Georges-Jacques Danton. 'You have thrown down the gauntlet to them, and this gauntlet is a king's head.' Yet the reality was that, for all the incandescent rhetoric on both sides, the more traditional impulses driving the war were revealed after the first French victory at Valmy on 20 September 1792.

The French army made its stand against the Prussians astride the road to Paris, a hundred miles from the capital. Fought on muddy ground, sometimes knee-deep in places, Valmy was primarily a lethal artillery duel, in which some 20,000 cannonballs were fired. The ragged French volunteers just held their nerve, a resistance that persuaded the Prussians, ravaged by dysentery, to retreat. In the despondent gloom later that evening, the great German writer Johann Wolfgang von Goethe gave some Prussian officers cold comfort by telling them that 'From this place, and from this day forth, begins a new era in the history of the world, and you can all say that you were present at its birth.' At first, Goethe's predictions seemed to come true: a second French victory, over the Austrians at Jemappes on 6 November, left Belgium open to French invasion. Intoxicated by this sudden reversal of fortune, the National Convention, the new republican assembly in Paris, issued the Edict of Fraternity on 19 November. This declared the Convention's intent to export the French Revolution, promising 'fraternity and help' to 'all peoples who wish to recover their liberty', meaning the overthrow of the existing order.

Yet, as French armies surged across the Low Countries, poured into the Rhineland, and, in the south, swept into Savoy (a duchy ruled by Piedmont-Sardinia which, with unfortunate timing, declared war on France the day after Valmy), the revolutionaries quickly set their principles aside. The occupied countries were too tempting a source of supplies and money for the French armies to leave simply to their own destinies. On 15 December, the Convention abolished the old regime in these territories, but in return the population were told to pay for the military costs of their liberation. The exploitation of conquests to fuel the French war effort was thus established at the very start, but such a ruthless policy could neither continue forever, nor resolve the problem of the people's political future. The revolutionaries soon articulated their objective: a defensible frontier, particularly in the north. It was Danton again who found the rhetorical flourish in January 1793: 'The limits of France are marked out by nature, we will reach them in the four corners of the horizon: the Rhine, the Ocean and the Alps.' On the suggestion of Dutch radical exiles in Paris, those territories overrun beyond these 'natural frontiers' would be converted into 'sister republics', exploitable satellite states allied to France.

Yet these conquests ensured that the war spiralled outwards. 'Natural frontiers' meant the annexation of Savoy, the Rhineland, and Belgium, plus a southern slice of Dutch territory. The logic of this last point meant war with the Netherlands, but the French invasion of the Low Countries also tensed to breaking point France's relations with the British, already strained by the overthrow of Louis XVI and by the Edict of Fraternity, which politicians feared might be applied to Britain, where there was an articulate and organized radical opposition. The French reopening to shipping of the River Scheldt, closed by treaty since 1648, also posed a direct strategic threat to the British Isles. If the French were to overrun the Netherlands, with its long North Sea coastline and boasting the fourth largest fleet in Europe, then the Royal Navy's capacity to defend home waters would be severely stretched. It was the French who actually declared war on both Britain and the Netherlands on 1 February. To make matters more desperate, they also opened hostilities against Spain on 7 March, effectively formalizing a rupture which already existed in fact: the Spanish had mobilized their forces in August 1792 (wisely pulling back from the brink after Valmy), but had then vigorously denounced the execution of Louis XVI (King Charles IV of Spain was also a Bourbon). The immediate consequence of the French victory in Europe was therefore to bind together one crisis—in relations between France and the German powers—with another long-term problem: the maritime rivalries of the western European powers, ensuring that the war would have a global impact across the world.

The most important of such repercussions were felt in the Caribbean, particularly Haiti. This, the most prosperous of all of France's colonies, burst into flames when its African slaves rose up in August 1791, well aware that government authority and the racial hierarchies of the French Empire had been fatally weakened by the Revolution. With the European conflict now engulfing the overseas empires, the Haitian Revolution became part of the global struggle: Spanish officials in neighbouring Santo Domingo immediately began supporting the insurgents as auxiliaries, while the British chose instead to back the white planters, who promised to submit to British authority in return for a restoration of slavery and protection against the insurrection. The French response was momentous: recognizing the reality that the Haitians had effectively liberated themselves, the Republic's commissioners in Haiti proclaimed the abolition of slavery, an act confirmed for the entire French Empire by the Convention in Paris on 4 February 1794. Slowly, cautiously, the Haitian revolutionaries, including one of their most charismatic leaders, Toussaint L'Ouverture, came over to the French side. The Spanish and the British, who invaded Haiti in September 1793, were driven back, the latter evacuating in 1798.

Back in Europe, the French Revolution was on the brink of collapse under the combined weight of the allied powers by the early spring of 1793. France was invaded across every frontier, north, east, and south. The Convention took the fateful step of imposing conscription, provoking open counter-revolution in western France in March, most notoriously in the Vendée, where, in a brutal civil war which did not end until 1800, the number of dead on both republican and royalist sides may have reached a horrifying 400,000. To war and counter-revolution were piled on the pressures of hunger, inflation, and the looming threat of popular insurrection in Paris. Overwhelmed, the Girondins were toppled by their Jacobin opponents in a coup d'état on 2 June 1793. France exploded into civil war, which the Jacobin government in Paris managed to crush and exact bloody retribution, but not before the French rebels in Toulon—the home of France's Mediterranean fleet—handed over their port to the British in August 1793. The young Napoleon Bonaparte commanded the artillery which finally drove them out in December. The Jacobins were able to master this intense crisis only through Terror, involving the arrest of 'suspects'; the trial and execution of people accused of treason; the summary execution of people found openly rebelling against the Republic; strict economic controls, backed up by draconian penalties; and, above all, the empowerment of the government to prosecute the war to the utmost. The *levée en masse* of 23 August requisitioned all adult males and all the country's resources in the first modern attempt to wage 'total war': there were close to a million Frenchmen under arms by the end of 1794, of whom perhaps three-quarters were combat-effective.

The war's dysfunctional pendulum finally swung back the other way on 26 June 1794, with a decisive French victory over the Austrians at Fleurus. A crushing British naval triumph over a French fleet in a battle remembered by the British as the 'Glorious First of June' could not dampen the renewed French impetus on the continent. With the tide of war turning, the Jacobin dictatorship was overthrown on 27 July 1794 (the Thermidor coup) and the Terror was over. Over the following year, the Convention drafted a new constitution, creating the Directory, which would govern France from October 1795: Bonaparte, still an artillery officer, prevented the Directory from being still-born, since his 'whiff of grapeshot' helped crush a royalist insurrection in Paris that month. He would destroy the same regime four years later.

Meanwhile, French armies had surged forward on all fronts, pouring into Belgium, the Rhineland, and northern Spain. In the deathly cold winter of 1794–5, the blue-coated hordes even managed to sweep into the Netherlands, since the waterways which usually provided the country's natural defences were frozen solid. So thick was the ice that in January the French cavalry thundered across the frozen sea to capture the Dutch fleet anchored at Texel: 'the first and last time—it can safely be assumed—that a naval engagement has been won by cavalry,' writes Tim Blanning. The balance of forces was tilting in France's favour. Prussia signed a peace treaty at Basel in April 1795, the Netherlands was turned into France's first 'sister republic' in May, and Belgium was formally annexed by France in October. Spain signed a peace treaty, also at Basel, in July 1795 and then this devoutly Catholic monarchy went so far as to enter an alliance with the godless French in August 1796. Spain, always caught in the crossfire in the Franco-British rivalry, saw in France the best hope of security for its extensive overseas empire. The French could now combine their fleets with those of the Dutch and the Spanish, while French control of the entire coastline from the Frisian Islands to Galicia strained the capacities of the Royal Navy. The British moved quickly to neutralize the most dangerous of these threats: the Dutch colony on the Cape of Good Hope, which was, the British commander who led the assault explained, 'a feather in the hands of Holland, but a sword in the hands of France', since it was the pivot of the sea route between India and Europe.

Yet the French were approaching a high-water mark in their success against Britain. In December 1796, an attempted invasion of Ireland was foiled when the French fleet was scattered by a storm. In February 1797, the danger still seemed so serious that there was a run on the Bank of England. The panic was becalmed that month when Admiral Sir John Jervis intercepted and destroyed a numerically superior Spanish fleet off Cape St Vincent as it was trying to link up with the French Atlantic fleet at Brest. The crisis was not over: in March, the French managed to land a motley band of deserters and adventurers on the Pembrokeshire coast. Although this, the last invasion of mainland Britain, was quickly mopped up, March and June saw mutinies break out in the Royal Navy at Spithead and the Nore, primarily over pay, rations, and conditions. These were suppressed with a mixture of executions and concessions, but it illustrated just how precarious Britain's situation was. The French and their allies tried to combine again in October 1797 when the Dutch fleet put to sea, but ran into Admiral Adam Duncan's ships off Camperdown: the dogged Dutch resistance only broke after nine ships of the line were taken. France's problems were compounded when the struggle for the sea spiralled into an undeclared naval war with the United States.

The war in Europe had strained French relations with the Americans, theoretically allied to France since 1778, when the old regime entered the American War of Independence. The United States, however, declared its neutrality in 1793: its armed forces were tiny and the British were the young republic's most important trading partner. Moreover, President George Washington was angered by the over-zealous French ambassador, Edmond Genêt, who armed privateers to sail from American ports against British shipping and who tried to whip up American public support for France. Yet the Americans also had grievances against the British: they harassed American shipping as they tried to throttle French commerce and seized sailors whom they suspected of desertion from the Royal Navy. The two countries nearly slid into war, until both sides pulled back from the brink in November 1794, when they resolved their differences in the Jay Treaty (named for the American diplomat involved), which effectively tore up the Franco-American alliance. The aggrieved French immediately launched privateering raids against American merchantmen: by June 1797, they had carried off some 316 ships. Although the two republics never formally declared war, they did exchange plenty of shots in anger on the high seas. An American effort at negotiation fell apart when it was learned in April 1798 that the slippery French Foreign Minister, Charles-Maurice Talleyrand, had tried to extract a bribe from the US envoys, who were approached by three agents known only as 'XYZ'. The quasi-war raged on.

If the French were frustrated at sea, they triumphed on land. A French assault in Germany floundered in 1796, but this was offset by a lightning strike into Italy by Bonaparte, now a general. Piedmont, its army outmanoeuvred and overwhelmed, sued for peace before the month was out. Bonaparte then moved against the Austrians, defeating them at Lodi on 10 May and entering Milan, the centre of Austrian power in Italy, five days later. The French had moved so quickly that they had easily outrun the other French thrust against Austria through Germany, so while waiting to strike northwards, Bonaparte raided central Italy, forcing Parma, Modena, and Tuscany to disgorge their hard currency. The Pope was not spared: the French invaded the Papal States—the Papacy's territorial domains in central Italy—and, at the Treaty of Tolentino in February 1797, forced the pontiff to yield some of his territory to France's new Italian sister republic, the Cisalpine, as well as some of his most cherished artworks, which were carted off to France and deposited in the Louvre. Then, having repulsed no less than three Austrian counter-attacks in the north, Bonaparte crossed the Alps and struck into Austria itself, entering an armistice at Leoben in April 1797. The peace treaty was finally signed at Campo Formio in October. The Austrians agreed to the French annexation of the left bank of the Rhine, the hard-won 'natural frontier', and recognized the Cisalpine Republic, in return for which Bonaparte, showing an almost casual regression to old regime balance of power ways, allowed Austria to annex Venice. The War of the First Coalition was over.

This was not a peace, but a stalemate: British and French negotiations in the summer of 1797 collapsed when a coup d'état in Paris in September (the Fructidor coup) purged the legislature and the Directory of moderate republicans and of real or suspected monarchists. The coup was a military intervention which set a dangerous political precedent—not least because it was Bonaparte who had provided the troops. The Directory was now led by hard-line republicans determined to pursue the war with more vigour and in this they had the wholehearted support of the generals. In the first months of 1798, the northern French ports saw a build-up of an 'Army of England' commanded by Bonaparte for the long-awaited descent on Britain. Yet the French could not control the Channel for long enough: the most they managed was to land 1,000 men in Ireland, in support of an insurrection which had erupted in May against British rule, arriving too late to make an impact.

By then, the war had thundered eastwards and engulfed another long-term challenge, the expansion of Russia. The Russian occupation of Poland in May 1792 and the Second Partition in 1793 naturally provoked Polish patriotism. After trying in vain to secure French support, Tadeusz Kościuszko proclaimed Poland in insurrection in Kraków in March 1794. After some early victories, the uprising crumpled under the sheer weight of Russian numbers. As the Russians closed in on Warsaw, the Prussians disengaged from the war against revolutionary France, which was not the easy 'promenade' they had expected, and instead sought a share of the territorial spoils in Poland. Even the Austrians, more committed than Prussia to the war in the west, were determined to have a slice of the conquests: they withdrew 20,000 troops from Belgium for operations against Poland, which both German powers invaded in June. After a slaughter which made the French Terror look amateurish (20,000 Poles were massacred in a single day on 4 November), the Russians took Warsaw. In the Third Partition between Russia, Austria, and Prussia, Poland was wiped off the political map in the New Year.

The War of the Second Coalition, 1798–1802

The wars in the east and the west were thus inter-connected, but were still to fuse into one single conflict. Yet the firestorm was gathering and, in 1798, it engulfed Russia and the Ottoman Empire in the War of the Second Coalition. The spark was Bonaparte's invasion of Egypt. This madcap enterprise was driven by two main concerns. First, it had become clear that Britain could not be defeated by an invasion or at sea, so the French had to find another way of challenging the British: Egypt would give them a base on the Red Sea, from where they might launch a strike on India. Secondly, an empire in the Middle East would compensate for the loss of the French Empire in the Americas. The French landed in Egypt in July 1798, stormed Alexandria, defeated the Mamluks who ruled Egypt in the name of the Turkish Sultan (at the Battle of the Pyramids on 21 July), and occupied Cairo three days later. Yet Bonaparte would not be triumphant for long: on 1 August, a British fleet under Admiral Horatio Nelson attacked and utterly destroyed the French fleet at Aboukir Bay. This victory persuaded the Ottoman Empire to fight, but, even more dramatically, Bonaparte's gambit brought Russia into the war.

The southward thrust of the French revolutionary armies in Italy had threatened Russia's strategic interests, since Russian shipping enjoyed access to the Mediterranean via the Black Sea. The situation became more alarming still when the peace at Campo Formio gave the French the Ionian Islands, which guarded the entrance to the Adriatic and were potentially a base for forays into the eastern Mediterranean, which Russia saw as its sphere of influence. The final straw was Bonaparte's conquest of Malta en route to Egypt, overthrowing the Knights of St John who had ruled the island since the sixteenth century and enraging Tsar Paul I, who had proclaimed himself the protector of their Order. The British triumph at Aboukir gave them all the final encouragement they needed.

The Austrians were also coaxed into taking up the sword and musket again. Bruised and battered though they were, the Austrians persisted in seeing France rampant as an intolerable threat to their strategic security. Although there were strong voices in Vienna that feared the costs of a further conflict against the revolutionary behemoth, the further wave of French aggression in the Mediterranean in 1798 spoke louder. Nelson's victory at Aboukir and a reassurance of Prussian neutrality persuaded Emperor Francis II that a further assault on French power was worth the risk. The alliance with Russia was sealed in September.

Yet before the Austrians and Russians could act on their military plans (an assault through Italy and French-occupied Switzerland into France), the first shots were fired in Italy in November, when the Neapolitans, also encouraged by Aboukir, struck northwards at France's Roman 'sister' Republic (created earlier that year). The result of this premature assault was a disaster: the French swept the Neapolitans aside, captured Naples, and established yet another republic in January 1799.

The Second Coalition finally responded with its own counterstroke in April. The Russian General Alexander Suvorov led the Austro-Russian forces to Milan within two weeks and swivelled southwards to rout the French in a relentless series of battles fought in blistering heat. The French reeled out of Italy, their defeat provoking a wave of popular insurrections. In the south, a 'Christian Army' led by Cardinal Fabrizio Ruffo crossed from Sicily and overthrew the Neapolitan Republic in the name of Church and King. In Tuscany crowds evoking the Madonna (shouting 'Viva Maria!') chased out the pro-French administration. These counter-revolutionary uprisings were not without their dark side, for the insurgents massacred the Jewish population in Siena. The allies struck into Switzerland and by June they were poised for an assault on France itself (see Figure 3). In August, the British and Russians launched an amphibious operation in the Netherlands, driving southwards towards Amsterdam.

The disaster provoked a domestic crisis in France which proved to be the making of Bonaparte. Counter-revolutionary uprisings broke out around Toulouse, while the Vendée was resurgent. Confronted with the twin threat of counter-revolution and an allied invasion, and desperate to avoid resorting to emergency measures which evoked the Terror, a number of moderate republicans decided that the time had come for strong government. They sought military support for their coup and Bonaparte appeared, having abandoned his army in Egypt, landed

3. As the artist intended, this heroic painting captures the determination of both Suvorov and his men as they pressed their offensive against revolutionary France in 1799

at Fréjus in October, and arrived in Paris. He led the Brumaire coup on 9–10 November, toppling the Directory, and, much to the chagrin of the politicians who had used him, assumed power as First Consul.

It was a propitious moment, for the tide was again turning in France's favour. The counter-revolution around Toulouse had been crushed and Bonaparte signed a peace treaty with the Vendée rebels in the New Year. The French had also driven the Russians back outside Zurich in September 1799, while the Russo-British expedition in the Netherlands got literally bogged down before being forced to withdraw in October. The Second Coalition split apart: the British wanted to force the French back to their old frontiers, the Russians intended to destroy the French Republic altogether, while the Austrians primarily sought to pluck the fruits of their conquests in Italy, as compensation for the loss of Belgium and the left bank of the Rhine. The British inflamed Tsar Paul when they captured Malta from its scurvy-wracked French garrison, but then showed that they had every intention of keeping this strategic gem for themselves.

Fulminating about his allies' treachery, Paul withdrew all Russian forces from the war in 1800, leaving the Austrians alone to face the French counter-attack. The Tsar, meanwhile, looked for ways of rattling the British. He forged a League of Armed Neutrality with Denmark, Sweden, and Prussia, which was aimed against British commerce in the Baltic (essential for its naval supplies) and which was encouraged by Napoleon, who also hoped to draw the United States into the agreement. At the end of 1800, Paul mustered 22,000 Cossacks in Central Asia and sent them southwards to attack the British in India. Although a damp squib, the expedition was the first ominous rumble of the nineteenth-century 'Great Game', the rivalry between Russia and Britain in Asia. The British, for the first time, became aware of the threat that Russia posed to their position in the subcontinent. While the dispatch of the first-ever British diplomatic missions to Persia and Sind (in present-day Pakistan) were initially provoked by the possibility in 1798–9 that Bonaparte might launch an overland assault towards India from Egypt, Russian southward pressure also entered their calculations. Paul's plans were cut short by his assassination in March 1801 at the hands of Russian court nobles, with (it now seems clear) the active support of the British secret service. The accession of his son Alexander I could not save the Danes—the front line of the League of Armed Neutrality—from British retribution. In April, a British expedition under Admirals Nelson and Parker shattered the Danish fleet at Copenhagen, before sailing into the Baltic and forcing the other members of the League to terms.

The Russian withdrawal from the European war was France's opportunity. Bonaparte crossed the Alps into Italy and defeated the Austrians at Marengo in June 1800. The Neapolitans were knocked out of the war in March 1801, while Portugal, invaded by France's Spanish allies, made peace in May. At the Treaty of Lunéville in February 1801, Austria acquiesced to all the French conquests made since 1792, while the British, exhausted, isolated, and with a change of government, opened the peace talks which led to the Treaty of Amiens in March 1802, ending the French Revolutionary Wars.

Chapter 3
The Napoleonic Wars, 1803–1815

The French Revolutionary Wars were over, but the peace of 1802 would prove to be only a truce. France and Britain were deadlocked, the Austrians battered and still threatened by a strong French position in Italy and Germany, the Russians had withdrawn in 1800 but were now acutely aware of the serious challenge posed to their vital interests by a resurgent France. Only Prussia had been clinging tenaciously to its neutrality since 1795, but a further French surge into Germany would change that. The Napoleonic Wars were therefore the final, deadly reaping of the long-term international tensions, frictions, and hostilities, seared together by the surge of French power in the 1790s. The peace treaties of 1801–2 did not secure a long-lasting peace because, first, Napoleon Bonaparte proved unwilling to accept even the expansive limits that they imposed on French hegemony and, secondly, because the British could not fully abide by the Treaty of Amiens without giving Napoleon the scope to ignore his own treaty commitments. The French position in Europe was indeed awe-inspiring: the French Republic now reached the Rhine, encompassing Belgium, Luxemburg, and the Rhineland; it stretched across the Alps, having annexed Nice and Savoy in 1793 and Piedmont in 1799. Beyond that, it held sway over a *cordon sanitaire* of 'sister republics', including the Netherlands, Switzerland, and, in Italy, the Ligurian (Genoese) and Cisalpine Republic (which Napoleon renamed the Italian Republic). This was, as the Director La Revellière-Lépeaux had once said, 'an uninterrupted continuity of territory…a nursery of excellent soldiers and a formidable position'.

The British, for their part, had to surrender all but a couple of the colonial conquests made overseas, including the Cape of Good Hope (to the Dutch) and Malta (to the Knights of St John). France was meant to surrender Egypt, but this had, in effect, already happened, since a British army had landed near Alexandria in March 1801 and took Cairo in June. The main territorial gains by the British occurred in South Asia, as an indirect result of the French invasion of Egypt. From the British East India Company's Indian headquarters in Kolkata, Bonaparte's thrust into the Middle East looked like the prelude to a descent on India. This was not mere paranoia: successive French regimes had sought ways of recapturing influence in India since their power had collapsed there during the Seven Years War. The British had mopped up the last remnants of French territory on the subcontinent in 1793, when East India Company forces overran the remaining French trading posts along the Indian coast, chief of which was Pondichéry. Yet the news of the French attack on Egypt, combined with intelligence that the governor of Mauritius, the French outpost in the Indian Ocean, had entered an alliance with Tipu, ruler of Mysore, provoked the British into action. The governor-general of British India, Richard Wellesley (older brother of Arthur, the future Duke of Wellington, then also serving in India), was bent on reducing Mysore, one of the great obstacles to British power on the subcontinent. The British invaded in May 1799, storming the citadel of Seringapatam, where Tipu's bullet-riddled body was found among a pile of corpses. The East India Company was now the pre-eminent, though not yet unchallenged, power in India.

Yet elsewhere the scale of the British concessions reflected the exhaustion of the country: if some hard-core British conservatives howled in protest, public opinion, sick of almost a decade of war, greeted the peace ecstatically. Moreover, diplomatic historians such as Paul Schroeder have argued that the Treaty of Amiens actually recognized the reality on the ground in that the three dominant powers were now Britain, France, and Russia. It might have held for longer than ten months had it not been, first, for the deep mistrust that continued to smoulder on both sides and, secondly, for the personality and ambition of Napoleon himself.

The illusion of peace

The trigger for the Napoleonic Wars was the relentless hostility between France and Britain. In Europe, the main British sin was to dally over evacuating Malta, as the peace treaty demanded. Yet the foremost problem was global: Napoleon still harboured ambitions to restore France as an imperial power and the European peace gave him the opportunity. The Spanish had ceded to their French allies the Louisiana territory, a funnel-shaped North American mass stretching from the Mississippi to the Rockies, with its point in New Orleans. Napoleon saw in this windfall the chance to rebuild an empire in the Americas. Louisiana would be a source of supplies for Haiti, which was now virtually autonomous under Toussaint L'Ouverture but which Napoleon wanted to restore to France. In late 1801, an expedition under General Charles Leclerc set sail with 7,000 men to destroy Toussaint's regime. Napoleon took the fateful decision to restore slavery in 1802, but the Haitians, bloodied after a decade of struggle, put up a gritty resistance. The French eventually poured 80,000 men into Haiti and captured Toussaint who died in the glacial Fort de Joux in the Jura in 1803. Still the Haitians prevailed: a lethal combination of military action and yellow fever finished off the French army. On New Year's Day in 1804, Toussaint's successor, Jean-Jacques Dessalines, proclaimed Haitian independence.

By then, war had erupted in Europe and Napoleon was ready to disengage from the Americas. The Directory had in fact already put out peace feelers to the USA before Bonaparte seized power in 1799, but it was the First Consul who signed the Convention of Mortefontaine in October 1800, formally burying the defunct Franco-American alliance of 1778. The French promised to respect American shipping, while the Americans waived compensation for damages to their vessels. Peace had been assured with the United States, but during the final days of the Amiens truce, as war with Britain loomed, so Napoleon took the most dramatic step of all: in May 1803, he sold Louisiana to the United States at a knock-down price.

Yet there were also signs that, instead, Napoleon was on the move in India. During the hiatus of the Amiens truce, he appointed one of his favourite generals, Charles Decaën, as governor of Mauritius, the Île Bonaparte (Réunion), and the French trading posts dotted around the Indian coastline, returned to France at Amiens. Soon after his arrival in Mauritius in September 1803 (and still unaware that France was again at war with Britain), Decaën tried to make contact with the Marathas, a mighty confederacy of Hindu warrior-princes in central India who now posed the greatest single challenge to British hegemony. They employed French mercenaries, including General Perron, who commanded 30,000 Indian and European troops. He was rewarded for his services to the Maratha prince, Sindia, with a fiefdom at Aligarh near Delhi. Decaën contacted both the Maratha leaders and Perron, urging them to fight the British. However Perron was no revolutionary, but an adventurer bent on making his own fortune. Yet for Richard Wellesley, Aligarh was nothing less than a 'French state erected... on the banks of the [River] Jumna'.

The British again responded by a pre-emptive strike. Perron's force proved to be a paper tiger, surrendering after Aligarh was stormed in August 1803. Yet elsewhere Maratha resistance was stubborn, combining the defence of formidable fortresses with attacks by light cavalry in the mobile warfare at which they excelled. They also used artillery (their gunners trained by Portuguese mercenaries) to devastating effect: when Arthur Wellesley won the Battle of Assaye in September 1803, it came at a cost of lives proportionately unmatched by any of his subsequent battles until Waterloo. The following year, the British suffered their worst-ever military disaster in India: a force deployed against Holkar, one of the Maratha leaders, was caught by the monsoon rains in central India in July before being routed by Maratha cavalry. The war dragged on until it fizzled out in the spring of 1805: the East India Company ran out of funds and its directors in London recalled an embittered Richard Wellesley who left India in August. Yet French hopes in India had been stymied.

These conflicts outside Europe kept Franco-British relations smouldering during the Amiens truce, but other European powers held deep anxieties about Napoleon. He blithely ignored his treaty commitments to withdraw French troops from the sister republics: instead, he became president of the Italian Republic and had himself appointed 'mediator' of the Swiss (Helvetic) Republic. Moreover, he engineered a surge of French influence in Germany in 1803 by virtually dictating the territorial compensations for the loss of the Rhineland. This involved 'mediatization', by which some German states absorbed the smaller principalities. In the process, the exuberantly complicated mess of 365 states in Germany were reduced to forty. Napoleon's aim was to strengthen those like Baden and Bavaria which, he calculated, would fall under French protection and act as allies against Prussia and Austria.

In May 1803, the flames finally burst when the British declared war. Napoleon had few ways in which to strike directly at the British. He built up a formidable invasion force on the Channel coast, but his other opening moves were almost guaranteed to invite the hostility of other great powers. Since King George III was Elector of Hanover, Napoleon sent his troops into the German state, inadvertently angering Tsar Alexander I, who was a guarantor of the Holy Roman Empire. He was also outraged by a French raid on the Duchy of Baden, in which a leading French royalist, the Duc d'Enghien, was snatched, carted back to France, and shot in the moat of the chateau at Vincennes. Even so, the Tsar dithered: a young ruler with liberal pretensions, he nourished some admiration for Napoleon, while there were some figures at court in St Petersburg who saw Britain, the tyrant of the seas and Russia's incipient imperial rival in Asia, as the greater threat to Russian strategic interests. For Alexander, however, the final straw came when Napoleon crowned himself Emperor of the French in December 1804: the general was now a usurper. Alexander sealed a formal alliance with the British in April 1805. Austria, although still recovering from the earlier war and financially desperate, joined this Third Coalition when Napoleon converted his 'Republic of Italy' into a kingdom with his stepson Eugène de Beauharnais as viceroy in Milan and extended direct French rule into Italy by annexing Genoa.

From Trafalgar to the Peninsular War

Dramatic and bloody though the Wars of the Third, Fourth, and Fifth Coalitions were between 1803 and 1809, the results of each merely strengthened the position of the three hegemonic powers. A Franco-Spanish fleet was torn apart on 21 October 1805 by the British at Trafalgar under Nelson (who died in the battle), but by then Napoleon had already turned inland to confront the Austrians and Russians. After an astoundingly rapid march through Germany, the French *Grande Armée* ensnared the Austrian army at Ulm in Bavaria on the day before Trafalgar, before driving eastwards, taking Vienna in November, and then swinging northwards to face a powerful Russo-Austrian army at Austerlitz in modern-day Slovakia. In what is considered their greatest military victory, on 2 December, Napoleon's men drove a wedge through the allies and routed them. Although the Russians regrouped and pulled out, the shattered Austrians signed a peace treaty at Pressburg, whereby they paid a large indemnity and surrendered all their Italian territory including Venice. By January, the British and the Russians were driven out of southern Italy and Napoleon's brother Joseph was put on the throne of Naples; in 1808, he was succeeded by the flamboyantly impetuous Marshal Joachim Murat. In 1806, the Batavian Republic was converted into the kingdom of Holland, with Napoleon's other brother, Louis, as its monarch.

That same year, the Emperor of the French announced the creation of the *Rheinbund*, the Confederation of the Rhine: the states of western and central Germany were torn out of the now moribund Holy Roman Empire, which the hapless Austrian Emperor Francis could only declare dissolved, ending a thousand years of history at the stroke of a pen. Assuming the role of 'mediator' of the *Rheinbund*, Napoleon's aim was to create a block of states allied to France, thrusting French power deep into the heart of Germany. This was enough to shake Prussia out of its neutrality and the Fourth Coalition was patched together when it allied with Britain and Russia. In Berlin, Prussian cavalry officers sharpened their sabres on the steps of the French embassy, but such confidence proved to be horribly misplaced. Without waiting for the Russians to arrive in strength, they struck against Napoleon in Saxony, where they ran into the French in October. While Napoleon mauled the Prussians outside Jena, on the same day Marshal Louis Davout's solitary corps held off the main body of their army near Auerstadt and routed them. With the shock of this double defeat, Prussian resistance crumbled and French troops marched through Berlin's Brandenburg Gate. They tramped straight on into Poland, provoking a Polish insurrection against Russian rule. A 30,000-strong force of Polish expatriates, some of whom had marched with Napoleon since his Italian campaigns, triumphantly entered Warsaw in November.

Napoleon's eastward advance rekindled the hopes of another Russian enemy, the Ottoman Empire. Napoleon gave them ample encouragement. An insurrection amongst the Ottoman Empire's Serbian subjects in the Balkans had erupted in 1804. Initially aimed only against the misrule of the Sultan's elite military caste, the Janissaries, the uprising effectively evolved into a war of independence. Napoleon, cultivating Turkish support against Russia, had condemned the Serbian revolution and, hearing of France's triumph at Austerlitz, the Turks had reciprocated by closing the Bosphorus Straits (linking the Black Sea to the Aegean) to the Russians. Russo-Turkish relations deteriorated over the course of 1806 and, with the French hinting that they would support an Ottoman reconquest of the Crimea, the Sultan declared war on Russia in December. The ensuing conflict lasted until 1812 and visited on the Balkans and the Caucasus the full horrors of ethnic cleansing, the slaughter of prisoners of war, and the massacre of civilians.

Meanwhile, Napoleon struck in the north. In February 1807, the French and the Russians clashed at Eylau in Poland. The snow-covered field was stained red with blood after a hideous slaughter from which the Russians withdrew in good order. Although usually described as a French victory, Eylau's real significance lay in the capacity that the Russians displayed to withstand the Napoleonic onslaught: it was a clash of two mighty empires, a foretaste of the kind of dogged opposition that Napoleon would later encounter from this particular foe.

In June, Napoleon struck again, this time decisively defeating the Russians at Friedland, persuading Tsar Alexander to ask for peace. Beaten militarily but not politically, Russia was not a power that Napoleon could handle with his habitual brutality. The negotiations between the two emperors, which opened on a raft floating on the River Nieman at Tilsit in July 1807, were a spectacle worthy of the great issues at stake. The importance of the Treaty of Tilsit was that it sought to carve Europe up into

French and Russian spheres of influence and tried to exclude Britain altogether. Russia annexed yet more of Poland (at Prussia's expense), while a secret clause gave Alexander the nod to invade Finland and wrest it from Swedish rule (which he duly did in a war in 1808–9). In return, Alexander agreed to join the continental blockade aimed against British commerce. Russia thus became a partner in France's domination of Europe. Beaten and shattered, Prussia was severely treated: its territory was dismembered, it was forced to pay a heavy indemnity, subsidize the French occupying army that patrolled the streets of Berlin, and reduce its own forces to a diminutive 42,000. Napoleon restored an approximation of Polish independence in the shape of the Duchy of Warsaw, whose territory was entirely taken from the Prussian partition. Its ruler was to be Napoleon's ally, Frederick Augustus, King of Saxony.

Napoleon's perennial headache, however, was how to defeat his most persistent of enemies, the British. Believing that he could throttle their economic and financial system by denying them export markets in Europe, beginning with the Berlin Decrees in November 1806 he tried to compel all his conquests, satellites, and allies to close their ports to British shipping. The entry of Russia into this 'Continental System' was a particularly serious matter, since it endangered British supplies of naval stores and grain from the Baltic. So the Royal Navy moved fast to prevent the Danes from joining the blockade, which would entirely bar their entry into the Baltic Sea. The British bombarded Copenhagen (with considerable loss of civilian life) and captured the Danish fleet in August 1807.

There was another gaping hole in Napoleon's blockade: Portugal. As the Danes were being pounded, the French warned the Portuguese to close all their ports to British vessels. Portugal's economy, however, was intimately bound to British commerce, so it could not comply. In the inevitably harsh retribution, a Franco-Spanish army invaded in November, sending Portugal's

Regent, Prince John, into exile in Brazil. Yet the looming presence of French troops along the supply routes across northern Spain began to chafe with their Spanish hosts. Although allies in name, the French forces began to look like an occupying army—and indeed they appeared suspiciously reluctant to relinquish the fortresses that they now held in the country. This precarious situation, as well as the lingering stench of defeat after Trafalgar, ricocheted against King Charles IV's chief minister, Manuel de Godoy, who was the unpopular architect of the French alliance. In March 1808 his opponents rose up at Aranjuez, the winter residence of the royal family, captured Godoy, and forced Charles to abdicate in favour of his more conservative but popular son, Ferdinand VII. Both sides now rushed to get recognition from the one ruler who could help their cause: Napoleon. The French Emperor agreed to meet the divided Spanish dynasty at Bayonne that April, but, in a brass-necked coup d'état, incarcerated the royals and gave the Spanish throne to his brother Joseph.

The response was almost immediate: on 2 May 1808, an uprising of Ferdinand's supporters in Madrid was crushed by the French, who killed up to 500 Spaniards, but the insurrection spread to the provinces, where insurrectionary juntas led the local resistance, eventually forming a Supreme Junta, first at Seville, until 1810 when the French would take the city, and then at Cadiz, where a parliament, the Cortes, would meet and, in 1812, proclaim a liberal constitution for the Spanish Empire. Some of the fiercest fighting in 1808 took place in Saragossa, where the Spanish fighters took to the rooftops and rained fire down on the French troops below. The Portuguese also rose up, proclaiming their loyalty to Prince John and driving the French from the countryside. The importance of the Portuguese uprising was that it gave the British their chance to open a European front against the French. A British army under Arthur Wellesley landed in August, linked up with the Portuguese army, and defeated Marshal Junot, who withdrew into Spain, where the uprising had developed into a guerrilla war. Although French strength was seeping out from this 'Spanish ulcer' (as Napoleon called it), they counter-attacked in 1810, forcing Wellesley (now the Duke of Wellington) back behind the formidable Torres Vedras fortifications protecting Lisbon. The British and Portuguese held out until March 1811, by which time disease and shortages of supplies had taken their toll on the French. They withdrew and in July 1812, Wellington was moving forward again, defeating the French at Salamanca and taking Madrid.

The global war

The war in the Iberian Peninsula had a global impact. Since the British army used gunpowder made from saltpetre gleaned from Bengal (which produced the best in the world), it was imperative that British sea routes across the Indian Ocean, still threatened by French privateers operating from Mauritius and Réunion, were secured. The British achieved this—and further tightened their grip on India itself—by taking the two islands in a series of amphibious operations in 1810.

The Peninsular War also created the immediate conditions in which Spain's empire in Latin America launched their bids for independence. There were, of course, distinctly American factors which created the groundswell, such as the evolution of colonial societies, the emergence of American identities, and sharp grievances with Spain's imperial rule, but few people in Latin America thought of making a concerted bid for freedom until after the Spanish crisis of 1808. The galvanizing impact in Latin America was remembered by none other than Manuel Belgrano, who would emerge as a leader of the Argentinian Revolution. He had fought against a British attack led by Commodore Home Popham, who, flushed with success after retaking the Cape of Good Hope from Napoleon's Dutch allies in January 1806, sailed across the Atlantic, and, in an unauthorized mission, occupied Montevideo and Buenos Aires. Belgrano led the colonial militia which beat off the invasion in 1807. A captured British officer remarked that the Argentinians had fought so well that they might consider political independence. Belgrano replied that the country was far from ready for such a drastic step. Yet, he later wrote:

> Such are the calculations of men! A year passed, and behold, without any effort on our part to become independent, God himself gave us our opportunity with the events of 1808 in Spain and Bayonne. Then it was that the ideals of liberty and independence came to life in America, and the Americans for the first time began to speak openly of their rights...

The war in Spain almost completely ruptured political relations between the metropolis and the colonies when, in 1810, the French nearly stamped their authority on the entire country. The first uprisings came that year in Argentina, Mexico, and Venezuela (where the revolution was led by Simón Bolívar and Francisco de Miranda: the latter had served with the French armies in 1792–3 and was imprisoned during the Terror). The Latin American Wars of Independence would rage mercilessly for the next twenty years.

Napoleon's attempts to barricade Europe against British commerce therefore had a world-changing impact—and it did not end with Latin America. The continental blockade caused friction between France and the United States, but the British response was even more chafing. In challenging neutral shipping that they suspected of trading with the Napoleonic imperium, they stopped and searched American vessels. Worse, the wear and tear on the Royal Navy as the war dragged on stretched its manpower and, in the process of forcing US merchantmen to heave to, they carried off sailors suspected of being British deserters.

So the same naval irritations that had brought Britain and the United States close to blows in the 1790s contributed to an actual war in 1812. The difference was that, this time, the Americans were determined to be more robust in their resistance: they had responded to British maritime depredations with a trade war, but, while inflicting economic misery on the US eastern seaboard, it made little impact on the British, who were busy exploiting the commercial opportunities offered by the Latin American bids for independence. The Americans therefore turned to strike at the British colonies in Canada, which they also hoped to conquer outright. The War of 1812 therefore broke out because of intransigence on both sides: the Americans because they set their sights on territorial expansion, and not only on righting their justifiable grievances at sea, the British because of their rough handling of neutral shipping. If the blame for the war was evenly shared, so too were the results: the American invasion of Canada in 1812 was a disaster and the British took Washington DC and burned it, but the Americans won an important naval victory on Lake Erie, defeated Britain's Native American allies (killing their inspirational leader Tecumseh), and—before news of peace between the two warring partners could reach the battlefield—repulsed an attempt by the British to take New Orleans in January 1815.

The defeat of the French Empire

In Europe, the war in Iberia had fused with a wider conflict, the War of the Fifth Coalition, which had been inspired in part by the Spanish resistance. Borne aloft by a resurgent wave of patriotic zeal, the Austrians mobilized against Napoleon. This culminated in clashes near Vienna at Aspern-Essling and Wagram, where the Habsburg forces led by Archduke Charles were defeated in July 1809. The immediate result was another Austrian humiliation: at the Treaty of Schönbrunn in October, the Austrians lost their Illyrian provinces (Slovenia and Croatia), which would be ruled directly from Paris; their ill-gotten share of the Polish partitions was divided between the Duchy of Warsaw and Russia and they were to pay an indemnity and cut their army down to 150,000 men. Napoleon even persuaded the Habsburgs to deliver up Archduchess Marie Louise, whom he married in 1810, to consolidate the enforced alliance between Austria and France and to give the Napoleonic Empire some dynastic respectability.

Yet, as Charles Esdaile has argued, the shattering of yet another Coalition, while an apparent triumph for Napoleon, also bore some serious if not immediately obvious signs that the military balance was tipping against him: the Austrians had inflicted no less than 50,000 casualties on the French and the ever-lengthening death toll of seasoned NCOs, army officers, and even generals had begun to tell in the way in which Napoleon was beginning to fight his battles. The tactics involved less and less the flexible formations for which French armies had been justly famous, and became increasingly reliant on the hammer-blows of frontal assaults by recruits hastily assembled and then poured into the cauldron of war. If French tactics from the very start had a high cost in human life, then after 1809, Napoleon's casualties became ever more appalling.

Nowhere was this truer than his ill-fated campaign against Russia in 1812. The Franco-Russian understanding was always fragile, but Napoleon's efforts to consolidate his authority in Europe eventually shattered it. In 1810, Napoleon annexed the Netherlands and north-eastern Germany onto the French Empire, to control Europe's maritime rind more directly, to reinforce the continental blockade, and to accelerate his attempts to rebuild a navy that could challenge the British. Yet in the process the Tsar's brother-in-law had been dethroned from the Duchy of Oldenburg. Alexander also suspected Napoleon of planning to restore a full-blooded Poland, which might threaten Russian security, especially when allied to the Ottoman Empire (which had been at war with Russia since late 1806, although peace was made in the nick of time in May 1812). Russia's economy suffered from the Continental System and the Tsar was under mounting pressure from the landowning nobility, whose prosperity was based on grain exports to Britain. Alexander responded by imposing heavy tariffs on imports from the Napoleonic Empire. While not a declaration of war, it was symptomatic of a wider collapse of the system established at Tilsit.

Napoleon amassed an enormous army of close to half a million men and invaded Russia on 24 June 1812. Yet the Russians had long understood that Napoleon relied on a rapid strike and the utter destruction of the enemy in a set-piece battle. For exactly that reason, wrote one of the Tsar's advisers, Russia had to 'plan and pursue a war exactly contrary to what the enemy wants'. And the strategy worked: the further that the main body of Napoleon's *Grande Armée*—375,000-strong—marched through choking dust and stifling summer heat through forests devoid of provisions and through charred villages, burned down to deny the invaders their resources, it haemorrhaged its strength through desertion, sickness, and the need to leave men to guard lines of communication, which were dangerously stretched. Yet the Russian commander, Mikhail Kutuzov, shrewd though he was, accepted that, politically, he could not surrender Moscow without serious resistance.

The bloodletting occurred at Borodino in September, in a slaughter graphically depicted by Leo Tolstoy. The Russians stoically stood their ground astride the Moscow road, blasted with artillery fire for most of the day (so much so, that on the Russian left flank, officers remembered that French cavalry charges were welcomed as a respite from the shelling). The Russian army eventually withdrew, depleted but intact, passed through Moscow, and regrouped to the south.

Napoleon enjoyed only a month in the Kremlin: the city around it was burned to the ground, probably by patriotic Russians at the instigation of Moscow's steely governor, Count Fedor Rostopchin. In October, the disastrous French retreat began, through a biting Russian winter that came early. While the Russians also suffered, mainly from problems of supply, Kutuzov kept up the pressure from behind, while Cossacks harried and picked off the French as they stumbled and froze to death through sub-zero temperatures (see Figure 4). Only 20,000 men out of Napoleon's main invasion force escaped.

The terrible defeat was a turning point: it devastated Napoleon's forces in the east and, while he was able to make good the hideous human losses, he never recovered from the dreadful death toll on the army's horses. Together, the Russian victory and the Spanish resistance galvanized the other European powers: the Russian invasion of Poland in the spring of 1813 spurred the Prussians, seething from the humiliations of Jena and Tilsit, to rise up against Napoleon. By June, the Sixth Coalition included Britain, Spain, Portugal, Russia, Prussia, and Sweden. Austria, suspicious of Russian intentions, delayed until Napoleon rebuffed the approaches by Clemens von Metternich, the Austrian Foreign

4. This engraving captures the exhaustion, suffering, and brutality that accompanied Napoleon's retreat from Moscow in 1812: in the foreground, freezing men are stripped and robbed while still alive, and a horse is butchered for its meat

Minister, for mediation. As the French withdrew into Saxony, the allied forces converged on Leipzig, where in the epic three-day 'Battle of the Nations' the French may have lost up to 100,000 men: in one particularly horrifying episode, a bridge was blown up while Napoleon's men were still retreating over it. French power in Germany now rapidly collapsed, and although Napoleon reached the Rhine with 100,000 men, they were weakened by typhus.

The Napoleonic Empire unravelled, as one state after another defected to the allies: only Murat, still King of Naples, remained loyal to his old master. The Swedes—now ruled by Bernadotte, one of Napoleon's former marshals—repaid French patronage by overrunning Denmark, a French ally, in December 1813–January 1814. The pincers closed in, as Wellington defeated the French at Vittoria in Spain in June 1813 and, in early 1814, invaded southern France. Further north, the allies crossed the French frontier. By March Russian and Prussian guns could be heard in Paris, where there was fighting at the very gates of the city. On 2 April, the Napoleonic Senate switched sides, proclaiming the restoration of the Bourbon monarchy, in the ample figure of Louis XVIII. Two days later, Napoleon abdicated, sailing for a comfortable exile on the Tuscan island of Elba. Yet he was not a man to enjoy peaceful retirement. In February 1815 he slipped back into France and marched on Paris, gathering supporters as he went. The King fled as Napoleon reached the capital in March.

These final 'Hundred Days' were the stuff of drama, but the European reaction is significant: its diplomats had already gathered at Vienna to begin their fraught yet groundbreaking negotiations to ensure that, this time, the peace would be a durable one. They digressed from their task to declare Napoleon an outlaw before returning to their main purpose. On the ground, meanwhile, Wellington brought together his British and Dutch forces in Belgium. The final collision occurred on the damp field of Waterloo, south of Brussels, on 18 June 1815, the arrival of the Prussians securing a decisive allied victory. His army shattered, Napoleon was soon captured, threw himself on the mercy of the British, and was exiled to St Helena, far removed from Europe.

Chapter 4
Total war, revolutionary war

> From this moment until that in which our enemies shall
> have been driven from the territory of the Republic, all
> Frenchmen are permanently requisitioned for service in the
> armies. The young men shall fight; the married men shall
> forge weapons and transport supplies; the women will make
> tents and clothes and will serve in the hospitals; the children
> will make up old linen into lint; the old men will have
> themselves carried into the public squares to rouse the
> courage of fighting men, to preach the unity of the Republic
> and hatred of Kings.

The Convention's decree of the *levée en masse* 23 August 1793 was
the ultimate expression of the 'nation-in-arms', the idea that, as
one revolutionary pithily put it in 1789, 'every citizen should be a
soldier and every soldier a citizen'. Customarily, the *levée en masse*
is taken to mark the transition from the limited warfare of the
eighteenth century to revolutionary war, in which an ideologically
motivated citizenry rallied to the cause of the French Revolution
and, against the odds, overcame the forces of the old European
order. 'War', wrote the Prussian soldier and military theorist Carl
von Clausewitz, 'had again suddenly become an affair of the
people, and that of a people numbering thirty millions, every one
of whom regarded himself as a citizen of the State... Henceforth
the means available... no longer had any definite limits... and
consequently the danger for an adversary had risen in the

extreme.' Yet historians have since wondered how far the secret of French success up to 1812 lay in this revolutionary mobilization of the people, in such terms as ideological commitment, new techniques on the battlefield, and the ability of the revolutionary state to dig deep into French society.

There was a clearly defined sense of both national identity and nationalism, which had been brewing in the decades prior to 1789 and truly fermented during the Revolution. French revolutionary nationalism was based on the idea that legitimate government could only arise from the French nation (which was why Napoleon crowned himself 'Emperor of the French' not Emperor of France) and successive regimes worked hard to fire up popular patriotism. In the process, they did mobilize much of the population into a gargantuan effort, particularly in the desperate years of 1792–4. In a phenomenon that would find its reflection among France's opponents as the wars intensified, such efforts certainly had some moral impact. The revolutionary feminist Théroigne de Méricourt appeared before the Convention, pistols in her belt, demanding the recognition of the Frenchwomen's right to form 'Legions of Amazons' to fight the war. Since women were denied political rights, a willingness to fight for the *patrie* was a way of claiming the full rights of citizenship. Male and female citizens collected 'patriotic donations' and presented them to the Convention for the war effort. There were cases of women donating their jewellery, in conscious imitation of the sacrifice of the ladies of ancient Rome, who in times of crisis gave up their finery for the sake of the state.

The *levée en masse* not only conscripted men into the army, but also explicitly mobilized all the resources of the country, recruiting thousands of workers and artisans to increase weapons and ordnance production. The Luxembourg Gardens in Paris resounded with the sound of hammers and bellows after they were converted into an open-air workshop for firearms.

Aristocratic mansions, convents, and even boats moored on the River Seine were similarly turned into manufactures. By these strenuous efforts, 5,000 Parisian craftsmen turned out 145,000 muskets a year, and one single factory churned out 30,000 pounds of gunpowder a day. In the ways in which the war effort reached deep into French society, through mass conscription, the mobilization of labour, and the ruthless exploitation of resources, this was not only 'total war', but also a people's war.

Such efforts at popular mobilization extended into the army. The civil authorities were determined that conscripts were fired up by patriotism and felt reassured that their sacrifices would be honoured by the *patrie*, the fatherland. Soldiers were reminded that they were citizens, not chattels: the revolutionary government insisted that soldiers had the right to vote and, on the eve of their departure, they were treated to civic banquets by the local authorities, who gave speeches on how the soldiers had the support of the very communities which they were defending. They were promised pensions on retirement, or on being invalided, while their families were assured that they would be supported for the loss of a breadwinner.

Yet the question as to how far the rank and file was actually driven by ideological fervour is an open one, not least because motivation is intangible and so hard to measure. One must ask, for example, how attentive nervous young conscripts actually were to local politicians lecturing them about the gratitude of the nation (see Figure 5). Yet the private correspondence of French soldiers, which their authors never intended for public consumption and so may be sincere, suggests that some were motivated by a strong sense of citizenship and patriotism. A letter from a young peasant soldier told his family that his life now belonged to the nation: 'either you will see me return bathed in glory or you will have a son ... who knows how to die for the defence of his country.' In the winter of 1793, another soldier had his faith in the liberating ideals of the Revolution confirmed when he saw enemy deserters coming over to the French side: 'They came across the river which is frozen over, because they no longer accept to be slaves, they want liberty.' After the victory, he added, the soldiers would share the laurels 'with our father, our mother, our brothers and sisters, and [in a nice Gallic twist] our mistresses'.

Yet these were the years of the Terror, when French soldiers and civilians were bombarded with republican propaganda and repeatedly warned of the dire, counter-revolutionary consequences of defeat. The Terror also worked in draconian ways to ensure that the army fought with determination: the central government and the representatives on mission, commissars sent from Paris to assert civil control over the armed forces, did not hesitate to execute commanders who they believed were less than zealous in their duties, an example which seems to have made a deep impression on the rank and file: in 1793–4, 84 generals were

5. Boilly's painting illustrates the conflicting emotions and mixed reactions of conscripts and their relatives

guillotined or shot, while 352 others were dismissed. These early years of the conflict were therefore exceptional and, while patriotism undoubtedly mattered in this period, most of the letters available to historians spoke only of fear, exhaustion, and despair. In June 1794, the conscript Pierre Delaporte wrote while fighting the British around Ypres:

> The law brought me to arms to defend my fatherland [*patrie*]
> which is dear to me. For it I have left my relations and fellow
> citizens who are also very dear to me…In doing my duty towards
> the one as to the other, I go to attack men whom I have never seen,
> who have done me no harm and who believe…that their cause is as
> good as ours…In these attacks, one often forgets, on both sides,
> all humanity.

Revolutionary nationalism may have shrivelled as many French soldiers became seasoned veterans and developed a professional ethos. Their loyalties shifted more to the army itself and, above all, to the inspirational commanders who had led them: Bonaparte was only one such figure. His men may still have been patriotically attached to France, but it was a loyalty expressed first and foremost through a soldier's professional pride and devotion to their great general. By the Napoleonic Wars, the French had travelled ideologically and morally a long way from the republican zeal of the citizen-soldiers of 1793.

One source of France's military strength may have lain in tactics, organization, and logistics. These were not entirely 'revolutionary' in that they originated from the Revolution. They were the product of old regime military theorists responding to the disasters of the Seven Years War. Before 1789, the royal army experimented at almost every level, from strategy and organization down to weaponry. Adopting the ideas of Pierre de Bourcet, a French staff officer who experimented with the deployment of independent columns in mountain warfare, and who published his conclusions in 1775, the army was redeployed into self-reliant divisions, each with its own infantry, cavalry, and artillery. Armies had customarily marched together along a narrower corridor of supply lines. The divisions of a French army would instead fan out and move across the countryside independently of each other, but maintaining regular contact. Each division was meant to be sufficiently strong to be able to hold off a larger enemy force until the other divisions came to the rescue by marching swiftly to the battlefield. By moving along separate routes, the French army could march rapidly, and in far greater numbers, living off the land and, ultimately, converging on the enemy army and destroying it. The Revolution adopted this concept and Napoleon enlarged the divisions into corps, each commanded by a marshal and coordinated by an efficient staff system: the textbook example of the strategy at work was the *Grande Armée*'s stunning surge through Germany during the Austerlitz campaign in 1805.

Once on the battlefield, the armies of the French Revolution put other old regime ideas into practice. For one, the French made skilful use of light infantry (*chasseurs*), deployed as skirmishers, sent out in small detachments with orders to reconnoitre the enemy, find weak spots, harass the opposition, offer a protective curtain as the main army deployed, and unsettle the enemy's by raking it with musketry (this was particularly effective at Jena in 1806). Such troops, operating away from the main body of the army and commanded by junior officers, had considerable scope for initiative, which gave them an ideological appeal to a French army reformed on the ideal of citizen-soldiers.

The French used artillery flexibly: it bombarded the enemy lines prior to the battle, but also, using the lighter guns introduced by the old regime expert Jean-Baptiste de Gribeauval, it would be moved to concentrate its murderous fire on weak points before the assault by infantry. While most eighteenth-century infantry generally attacked in lines, deployed abreast, to maximize firepower, an assault by a French revolutionary army came in columns: narrow in the front, but deep, so that one rank hurtled on after another, sacrificing firepower in favour of shock. Lines of infantry were deployed to protect the flanks with their musketry, so French tactics were called the *ordre mixte*, the 'mixed order' of column and line, which had been conceptualized by another old regime theorist, Jacques de Guibert, in 1772, but became the standard form of deployment in the new army regulations of 1791. Once the columns had broken through the enemy, cavalry would surge through the gap and break their army apart.

The use of these tactics, where an enemy was hit hard and fast, led the French to emphasize victory in a decisive battle which destroyed the opponent's army. This was a critical strategic difference between the conduct of 'revolutionary' and old regime warfare: the professional armies of the eighteenth century were expensive and conflict so frequent that commanders aimed to fight a war of manoeuvre, threatening the enemy's lines of communication and forcing a negotiated peace, rather than waste human lives and materials in the carnage of a great battle. The contemporary British expert General Henry Lloyd wrote that such wars could be waged with 'geometric strictness', allowing an army to 'wage war without ever finding it necessary to be forced to fight'. The French revolutionaries and Napoleon alike behaved very differently.

Essential to their energetically aggressive tactics was determined, dynamic leadership willing to strike ruthlessly when the opportunity arose. The French Revolution provided this leadership by its reforms back in 1789. Napoleon is meant to have said that every French soldier carried a marshal's baton in his knapsack, but the more prosaic truth was just as impressive: by opening promotion to the officer corps to all men—and not, as before 1789, exclusively to the nobility—the French Revolution released cohorts of experienced men from the ranks into the officer corps: less than 5 per cent of officers up to the grade of captain in 1800–14 were from the old nobility. At least 67 per cent of the 2,248 generals in the French army between 1792 and 1814 were of non-noble origin. Of Napoleon's eighteen marshals in 1804, only five could claim to be of noble blood. Lannes came from the peasantry, Augereau's father was a domestic servant, and Murat, King of Naples between 1808 and 1815, was the son of an innkeeper. In the army, at least, the revolutionary principle of 'careers open to talent' was no myth. The experience of such promotion in other European armies was not unknown, but not as common. In Russia's Preobrazhensky Guards, 6 per cent of the officers were sons of soldiers, labourers, or peasants who had proved themselves on the battlefield. The British army drew hundreds of British officers from the well-heeled gentlemen who had served in the militia, giving young middle-class men an opportunity for promotion which otherwise they might never have had. Five per cent of British officers had risen from the ranks because of bravery or long service, but 20 per cent of commissions were still purchased and promotion within the officer corps often depended on political connections, favouring the gentry.

Leadership was no doubt a vital ingredient of the persistent French success on the battlefield and nowhere was this more visible than at the top: Napoleon was not the only French commander who was inspirational, aggressive, and gifted with what contemporary theorists called the 'coup d'œil', an eye for the right moment at which to strike. Young and determined to prove their mettle, they led from the front. These qualities prompted Theobald Wolfe Tone, the Irish republican leader who was in France between 1796 and 1798, to comment that 'If a man will command French troops, he must be *rather* brave…the French Generals not only gave the *command*, but the *example*, to their soldiers. They are noble fellows, that is the truth of it.' Where Bonaparte excelled was in using a mixture of personal example, propaganda, honours, and chastisement to motivate his soldiers. He led from the front in Italy in 1796–7, sharing the dangers with his men; he worked hard to ensure that his army was adequately paid and provisioned, even if that meant picking the plains of Italy bare to do so; he gave out engraved sabres to men whose courage caught his attention; but he scolded soldiers who he thought had failed in their duty: 'Soldiers, I am not happy with you...Soldiers of the 85th and 39th', he roared at two units who broke and ran in 1797, 'you are no longer French soldiers.' The offending troops responded by pleading for a chance to redeem themselves and, in the next clash, took very heavy casualties.

Finally, he made masterful use of propaganda to create a personal mystique of his genius as a commander, both amongst his troops and at home. The *Courier of the Army of Italy* was distributed gratis amongst the soldiers in the field and the civilian population in France: Bonaparte penned a lot of the articles. In one utterly shameless passage, he wrote of himself: 'He promised victory, and brought it. He flies like lightning, and strikes like thunder. The speed of his movements is matched only by [the soldiers'] accuracy and prudence. He is everywhere. He sees everything. Like a comet cleaving the clouds, he appears at the same moment on the astonished banks of two separate rivers.' As the historian David Bell has suggested, this was not just propaganda, but the creation of a personality cult based on a subtle blend of myth, real skill as a commander, and adept use of the personal touch. On the eve of battle, he would wander around the soldiers' bivouacs, asking after their well-being and encouraging them for the combat the next day. A veteran of Austerlitz later wrote, 'The presence of the emperor produced a powerful effect on the army. Everyone had the most implicit confidence in him; everyone knew, from experience, that his plans led to victory, and therefore...our moral force was redoubled.'

Yet some historians have asked whether the differences between the French army and the rest were as decisive as was once thought. For one, old regime armies did use skirmishers and light infantry, even if not with the same legendary zeal as the French. In the 1790s, Prussian fusiliers were trained to engage French skirmishers in the kind of open warfare that the latter excelled in—and their discipline was based less on punishment than on their professionalism and unit pride. The Austrians had Tyrolean sharpshooters (although their privilege was to serve only in their own province) and Croatian light troops, while the Russians boasted no less than 30,000 trained skirmishers (*Jaeger*) in 1789. This number had swelled considerably by 1812, although Russian officers always had misgivings about the wisdom of giving serf conscripts such room for personal initiative. The Russians could also call on the Cossacks, who as light cavalry played a role similar to the skirmishers. The French artillery reforms, both in terms of the technical specifications of the guns (increased mobility, greater standardization) and their deployment on the battlefield, had been adopted from Prussian practice: as French attaché to the Austrian army during the Seven Years War, Gribeauval had been on the receiving end of such devastating gunnery.

In any case, most armies evolved in response to the long war: by 1812, the British probably had the best single light infantry formation in Europe (the Light Division serving in Spain), while the Russians may have had the best horse artillery. Secondly, coalition forces eventually learned that, since Napoleon's strategy depended on the utter destruction of his opponents in a collision on the battlefield, the best means of defence was not to oblige him: in Spain in 1810, the British, Portuguese, and Spanish showed how strategic withdrawal, leaving scorched earth behind them, could exhaust the French, before the allies struck back in 1812 and again in 1813. The Russians watched the war in Spain with interest and, as early as March 1810, were drawing up plans for such a strategy in the event of a French invasion. In August 1811, Tsar Alexander I told the Austrian government that 'It is only by being prepared, if necessary, to sustain war for ten years that one can exhaust [Napoleon's] troops and wear out his resources'. But to do that, a state had to have a deep or rugged hinterland to retreat into: it is no coincidence that Napoleon met his most disastrous defeats in Russia and Spain. Finally, some historians have pointed to the critical factor of numerical superiority. French battlefield tactics involved appalling casualties, possibly because the key to French success was less any tactical finesse than their ability to throw numerically superior forces into the carnage until they overwhelmed the opposition by sheer force of numbers. When the allies managed to match them man for man, the French lost. The key to French victory, and Napoleon's ultimate defeat, therefore lay in the efficiency with which the opposing sides could mobilize their human and material resources.

On paper, the successive coalitions ought to have had a decisive advantage. France, as the contemporary military theorist Clausewitz noted, had a population of close to 30 million at the outbreak of the French Wars, which was easily outnumbered by the Russian Empire alone, which had 40 million. Combined with France's other main opponents in this period—Britain (15 million), the Habsburg Empire (22 million), and Prussia (10.7 million)—the allied powers had an overwhelming advantage in purely demographic terms. Yet no matter how populous and prosperous a country might be, for any state to prosecute a war, a government needs the mechanisms to tap the human, financial, and material resources embedded within society. While inspired strategy, tactical brilliance, and acts of bravery can decide individual battles and campaigns, an entire conflict is ultimately decided not only by the overall balance of numbers, but also by the ability of the belligerents to exploit their resources effectively. Warfare is not just a question of what happens on the battlefield, but also of how to secure the men, money, and supplies needed to keep fighting.

Occupied Europe and the Napoleonic Empire

For all the might of France itself, such was the scale of the conflict that French resources alone were never enough to allow Napoleon to wage war with all its dreadful human costs. The solution was to exploit the Napoleonic Empire, which fell into three zones. First, there was the 'Empire of the French', ruled directly from Paris, which at its height in 1811 included France and the Low Countries; the Rhineland, Hamburg, Bremen, Lübeck, and Oldenburg in Germany; Piedmont, Genoa, Parma, Tuscany, and Rome in Italy; and Illyria (modern-day Slovenia and Croatia). Secondly, there were the satellites, which were notionally independent, but which were in fact puppet-states ruled by Napoleon, his family members, his marshals, or other appointees, including Westphalia and Berg in Germany, the Italian kingdom of Naples, Switzerland, and the Duchy of Warsaw. Thirdly, there were countries whose rulers calculated that their interests were best served by an alliance with France, like Denmark, Baden, Bavaria, Württemberg, Saxony, and those who had been bludgeoned into joining Napoleon, namely Prussia in 1807 and Austria in 1809.

The primary purpose of such domination was to feed the war effort with cannon fodder, money, and material resources. During the French Revolutionary Wars, metal currency was extracted from the occupied territories by draconian financial levies: between September 1794 and November 1798, millions of *livres* were sucked out of the Rhineland, including a heart-stopping 50 million in December 1795. Italy fared little better: in 1796, Parma was emptied of 2 million *livres*, Genoa 2 million, and Milan a crippling 20 million (five times its usual annual tax revenue). Ordinary people suffered the most, since official demands for money came on top of requisitioning of supplies by French soldiers. On top of this, the conquests, whether annexed to France or converted into 'sister republics', were bound to raise soldiers, either as conscripts directly into the French army, or in their own forces, which were deployed in French interests.

Yet where the French were able to put down institutional roots, particularly in the inner parts of Napoleon's Empire—Belgium, the Rhineland, Piedmont—they left a constructive legacy. The abolition of seigneurialism and serfdom, and the principles of civil equality and meritocracy explicit in the Napoleonic Code of 1804, were introduced across the Empire and in the satellite states, while the religious toleration written into the Concordat of 1802—whereby Napoleon made peace with the Catholic Church after more than a decade of revolutionary conflict in France—was rolled out across his European empire, often against the bitter, violent opposition of the zealously orthodox. Yet, fundamentally, the three spheres of French domination were exploited for their human and material resources.

It all began, however, with France itself. When Bonaparte seized power in 1799, he inherited a French state which had undergone a decade of revolutionary reform. Napoleon's inheritance included the efficiency of France's new administrative system, a centralized, uniform structure of which the Bourbon monarchy could only have dreamt. The French Revolutionary Wars had showed just how effective the system could be in mobilizing French society. In 1789, the overlapping and often conflicting jurisdictions of royal officials, sovereign courts, and provincial institutions were abolished, and replaced by eighty-three more or less equal departments, which became (and remain) France's main administrative unit. While initially the purpose was to *de*centralize by placing local initiative into the hands of elected officials, the current could be reversed, so that authority could flow from the centre and be imposed, via the departments, onto the districts and communes (the most localized level of authority).

While the Revolution began this process of centralization, it reached its apotheosis under Napoleon, who in 1800 introduced the prefects, one for each department. They were the eyes, ears, voice, and hands of the central government, charged with public order and the enforcement of all the laws coming from Paris, while reporting back on the condition of their departments. Lucien Bonaparte, Napoleon's brother and his first Minister of the Interior, admonished the first prefects with a long list of duties, at the top of which they were to 'apply yourself immediately to the conscription draft... I give special priority to the collection of taxes: their prompt payment is now a sacred duty.' As the 'Empire of the French' expanded, so too did this administrative system: by 1811, it stretched from northern Germany to Rome, incorporating a grand total of 130 *départements*, each with their own prefect.

Dramatic though the *levée en masse* of 1793 was, the conscription system that Napoleon inherited from the Revolution was the Jourdan Law of 1798, which remained in force until 1815. Every 22 September (the first day of the year in the Revolutionary Calendar, which Napoleon did not abandon until 1806), all young men of 20–5 years of age were arranged into 'classes', from which the new conscripts were drawn by lot, beginning with those aged 20 and then progressing up the age scale as required. As the 'Empire of the French' expanded, so too did the Jourdan Law: by 1811, recruits from as far north as the German Hanseatic ports and as far south as Rome were being directly conscripted into the French army. Only Illyria was exempt, because this region was the old frontier with the Ottoman Empire and the Croats had a tradition of military service in return for land and personal freedom. Napoleon's satellite states and allies were also required to raise armies, a 'blood tax' which was resented, often evaded, and sometimes resisted, but which meant that Napoleon's forces were polyglot: two-thirds of all his troops came from outside France proper, including Poland, Lithuania, Croatia, Germany, Switzerland, Italy, the Low Countries, and Spain. From the Emperor's perspective, the system meant that he could rely on a steady supply of recruits: the levies from France alone between 1800 and 1813 raised 2.8 million men. At the hideous sight of thousands of frozen corpses at Eylau, he is meant to have said, 'I have an annual income of 100,000 men; one night in Paris will replace this.' After 1812, however, as the Empire unravelled and more and more of the burden of fighting fell on the French themselves rather than their allies and satellites, the system became utterly rapacious in France. One of Napoleon's prefects bluntly complained in 1813 that 'I am taking everyone; there will be no one left from the years 1813 and 1814 capable of procreation and maintaining the population': by this point, nearly 50 per cent of each class were being drafted. In all, 7 per cent of the entire French population was conscripted under Napoleon (36 per cent of all those liable).

Also essential for France's military capacity, the Revolution had decisively sliced through the knot of fiscal privilege, venal offices, and tax-farms which had proved so resistant to reform prior to 1789. In its place was put a system of direct, uniform taxation based on incomes and land, to which were later added indirect taxes on consumption and on the employment of domestic servants, coaches, and windows. The revolutionaries also raised, potentially, some 2,000 million *livres* from the nationalization and sale of church land. At the same time, the revolutionaries, adherents of the free market that they were, had eliminated the morass of internal customs barriers and tolls and banned such restrictive institutions as guilds. In France, Napoleon therefore inherited the makings of a resurgent economy tapped by an effective fiscal system—one which he then fine-tuned by introducing a comprehensive tax survey and further indirect taxes on such consumables as tobacco, alcohol, and salt. He also established the country's first national bank, the Bank of France, in 1800, with shareholders and government backing, although the attempt to mimic the British 'sinking fund' to manage the national debt failed because investors were wary of buying its interest-bearing bonds.

The French system of public finance was introduced across Europe to varying degrees, but, vast though the amounts of money raised were, they never met the spiralling costs of the war: the kingdom of Italy's tax revenues were boosted by 50 per cent between 1805 and 1811, but its debts *quintupled* in the same period. Almost everywhere, the authorities tried to make up the shortfalls by increasing indirect taxes—on salt, tobacco, and imports—but since these fell proportionately harder on the poor, they provoked seething resentment.

The exploitation of Europe took a particularly sophisticated shape in the 'Continental System', established by the Berlin decrees in November 1806. The aims of the system were twofold: to wage economic warfare on the British by excluding their commerce from Europe and to secure a captive market for French agriculture and manufacturing. This latter goal—which has been described as the 'uncommon market' or a 'one-way common market'—was only partially met. Some European economies certainly profited from the system: with British imports slowing, the cotton manufacturers of Saxony and the wool weavers of Silesia were able to export to Eastern Europe, while some historians have argued that Belgium witnessed its first great period of industrial 'take-off' behind the blockade's protection. Yet Napoleon himself was adamant that his economic watchword was *la France avant tout*—'France first'.

In practice, some parts of France benefited while others suffered desperately. Profiting from its strategic location on the Rhine, Alsace became an important entrepôt for commerce between the French Empire proper and the satellite states in Germany, but the life was stifled out of the maritime ports and their hinterland, suffering from the lack of overseas trade and of imports of raw materials. In 1808, the American consul at Bordeaux wrote that 'grass is growing in the streets of this city. Its beautiful port is deserted except by two Marblehead fishing schooners and three or four empty vessels which still swing to the tide'. It is perhaps no surprise that as the Empire collapsed in 1814, Alsace remained loyal to Bonaparte, while the Bordelais welcomed Wellington as a liberator.

The aim of sinking British manufacturing floundered because the system was never watertight in barring British goods: it could only work if Napoleon was able to offer his European subjects alternatives to imports from Britain and its empire, but he could not. The European demand for commodities such as sugar, coffee, and cotton was such that it could only be fully satisfied by tapping the global trade that the British dominated. The British happily

6. Public bonfires of British contraband, like this one in Amsterdam in 1812, were aimed at reinforcing Napoleon's blockade of Europe, but they also appalled mercantile communities already suffering from the commercial disruption of the 'Continental System'

obliged by setting up smuggling centres on Gibraltar, on Mediterranean islands such as Corfu, Sicily, and Malta, and on Heligoland in the North Sea: sugar from the British plantations in the Caribbean was spirited ashore at Salonika and furtively carried over the mountains by mules, before being sold across the Napoleonic Empire. In 1812, Napoleon appalled Europeans by ordering public bonfires of millions of francs worth of confiscated British contraband in Amsterdam, Hamburg, and Frankfurt (see Figure 6). Yet the French themselves realized Britain was an important market for their wine, champagne, brandy, silk, even wheat, and the Napoleonic state periodically issued licences permitting its subjects to trade with the British in such goods. The most devastating consequence, however, was political: to enforce the blockade, Napoleon resorted to political pressure and, on two particularly fateful occasions, to force: the first of these was when he attacked Portugal in 1807, precipitating the agonies of the Peninsular War, and the second was the equally disastrous invasion of Russia in 1812.

Chapter 5
Soldiers and civilians

The horrors unleashed by the French Wars were captured in the stark, disturbing prints of the Spanish artist, Francisco Goya. *The Disasters of War*, their dark lines etched in 1810–20, freeze in time the agonies and brutality of the guerrilla war in Spain: women being raped, the limp corpses of civilians dangling from gibbets, a priest garrotted, a soldier on the verge of having his head cleaved in two by an axe. There are no heroes or villains: in some of these etchings, it is impossible to distinguish between Spanish guerrilla and French soldiers, between aggressor and victim. The violence is indiscriminate, senseless, but therein lies the horror: anyone could become a victim, at any time (see Figure 7).

The French Wars all but shattered the eighteenth-century notion that there were 'rules' to warfare. The Swiss jurist Emmerich de Vattel, whose 1758 work *The Law of Nations* was an influential attempt to outline the rules of conduct ('the proper form') of international relations in war and peace, including the definition of a 'just war' and the treatment of civilians and property, wrote that 'the Nations of Europe almost always carry on war with great forbearance and generosity'. Such ideas were overlaid by the cosmopolitanism of the Enlightenment—the idea that all people shared such fundamental attributes as reason and certain rights and were governed by similar, natural laws. The total wars of the French Revolution and Napoleon did not, however,

7. Goya's 1810 etching captures the appalling waste of life during the Napoleonic Wars. The nationality of the victims is unclear, as is whether they are soldiers or civilians—all powerfully suggestive of the indiscriminate nature of the horrors of war

only destroy these illusions because of their stark brutality. It was also that there was a dangerous contradiction within the Enlightenment's humanitarianism. Within that body of ideas there lurked a sinister virus: what of those who did not conform to the 'rules' that limited warfare? What of people such as rebels, guerrillas, bandits, or non-European 'savages' who fought a different type of warfare from the set-piece battles envisaged by the eighteenth-century jurists? And what of states deemed by their opponents to have breached the laws of warfare, or to be waging an 'unjust' war? Vattel himself provided the answer: they were 'monsters' who could be exterminated.

The soldier's war

The ultimate price of suffering and death was paid by the soldiers, sailors, and civilians who found themselves in the line of fire. Everywhere in Europe, a soldier's first encounter with the army was at recruitment or, more often, conscription. The burden of military service fell upon the poorest, because those with money could pay for someone to join the ranks in their stead. Only France periodically prohibited such substitutions, under the *levée en masse* of 1793 and the Jourdan Law of 1798, but Bonaparte, believing that the educated and the monied would serve him better as officials and taxpayers, reintroduced the practice. French conscripts were to serve until the peace, which in the event translated into many hard years of campaigning.

In Britain, the army was never popular amongst civilians: although the government experimented with short periods of service, enlistment was for life, officers arguing that a recruit had to be forced to break decisively with civilian life. Yet it was precisely for this reason that service was unpopular, in a society where workers and artisans expected to sell their labour freely and, if they were skilled, command high wages for it. In 1787, the Adjutant-General complained that 'the miseries of the soldier's situation' made it 'impossible to suppose that any eligible man in his sober senses will enlist as a soldier'.

Conscription was a traumatic experience for any civilian, but nowhere was it more so than in Russia, where the 20 million serfs bore the brunt. Responsibility for choosing the recruits ultimately fell on the village elders, who, although serfs themselves, invariably selected people whom they regarded as troublemakers and misfits. Russian conscripts were fated to serve for twenty-five years without leave, which was effectively a life term: such was the waste of human life through disease and combat, that only 10 per cent survived that long. In a society where less than 5 per cent of the population was literate, a soldier did not write home. He rarely, if ever, saw his family again, since those who returned, forgotten, scarred, or maimed, were treated as outcasts. A Russian conscript was therefore dead to his family: his beard and hair were shaven off, since he was no longer considered a villager, and on the eve of the departure, his family would hold a wake. When the time came, the conscript would be accompanied to the village limits by his family and friends, singing funereal songs. They then turned their backs on the recruit, as if he were already dead. If a conscript left behind children with no one to look after them, they were sent to military orphanages, where they were trained to be NCOs: conditions here were so harsh that a third never lived to see adulthood.

Unsurprisingly, civilians made determined efforts to avoid conscription. The most obvious way was desertion. Some potential French recruits tried to evade service by simply failing to register for the draft, but for those actually conscripted the best chance of desertion was on the march to the military depots, since the local territory was familiar. Eugène de Beauharnais, Napoleon's stepson and regent in the kingdom of Italy, estimated that a third of the deserters absconded just after being recruited. The incidence of desertion across Europe varied for many reasons: it was easier to escape the army in areas which were mountainous, densely forested, or frontier regions. In the Russian Empire, the distances were so vast and a runaway conscript so obvious that desertion was a very risky undertaking, but when the Russians invaded Europe, their soldiers had more opportunity to escape. Desertion actually increased when a Russian unit received orders to return home, since conscripts knew that their chances of flight would recede once back on Russian soil.

Language was important, too: on Napoleon's side, troops who did not speak French were more likely to desert than francophone soldiers. The rates of desertion also varied from year to year: in the French Empire, they fluctuated according to the regime's capacity to repress it. In France, desertion rates were higher when the state was weaker, particularly in the later 1790s, when the Directory was lurching from one crisis to the other, and again when the Napoleonic regime was under the cosh from 1813 and when demands for troops fell heavily once again on the French themselves. In between, however, desertion rates plummeted to as little as 2 per cent in some areas. French deserters sometimes formed gangs to rob isolated farms and travellers: this may have been pure banditry, but it was sometimes harnessed by royalists and directed against government officials and supporters of the revolutionary order. Everywhere in Europe, deserters had a better chance of escape and survival where they were supported by their own community, hiding them from the police and keeping them fed and sheltered.

Entire communities might also resist conscription by rising up in riot or rebellion. The creation of a militia in Ireland in 1793 led to outbursts of violence amongst the peasantry, while extra levies sparked riots in England in 1796 and Scotland in 1797. If such violent opposition arose against service in a force intended only for home duties, then it is scarcely surprising that conscription for the line army could provoke full-blown revolt. In areas under French domination, insurrection was often stoked by other grievances, such as the misery of life in a war zone, social disruption caused by invasion, and the revolutionary attack on the Church, but the introduction of conscription was often the final trigger. In France in 1793, conscription sparked the counter-revolution in the Vendée, Normandy, and Brittany, areas where feelings were already raw with hostility to the Revolution. When the Jourdan Law was imposed by the French government on Belgium in September 1798, the country, already seething against the Revolution's other reforms, exploded in a 'peasants' war', a rural uprising which was brutally suppressed by year's end. Opposition was particularly determined in regions—like Belgium—which were unaccustomed to conscription. When the Tyrol, part of the Habsburg Empire customarily exempt from conscription, was annexed by Napoleon's ally Bavaria, which then introduced the draft, an insurrection in 1809 led by Andreas Hofer—an innkeeper and horse trader—succeeded in taking the provincial capital Innsbrück. Hofer waged a guerrilla war until a Bavarian counter-offensive, boosted by French forces, crushed the uprising. Hofer was captured and shot by firing squad.

Such open insurrections occurred in European regions already deeply hostile to the political order. Yet for the majority of Europeans, there were subtler ways of evading recruitment. Where members of a community were well liked, or valued for their skills, the locals rallied around. In Britain, people pooled their money to pay for substitutes for people they did not want to lose to militia service. In France, local authorities protected their own by loosely interpreting the term 'unfit for service', although the Napoleonic regime soon grew wise to this and thrust responsibility for conscription onto 'recruiting commissions' of prefects and military officers. Marriage was another way out: in the Napoleonic kingdom of Italy, young men married women old enough to be their grandmothers, since under the French system a married man was classified as 'the last to march'. More drastic measures included self-mutilation—men hacked off their index fingers so that they could not pull a trigger, or they had their teeth pulled out so that they could not bite off the seal of the cartridges needed to fire their muskets.

The surviving correspondence of French soldiers shows that those who would not, or could not, evade conscription went through a range of tortuous emotions: loneliness after being cut off from family and home, confusion as they adjusted to an alien way of life, boredom in the barracks or camp, and anxiety as they confronted the possibility of death. Comrades were therefore essential, for they shared the same hardships, offered sociability and company around the camp fire or cooking pot, and swapped stories, sang songs, and shared jokes: these are not idealizations of army life, but were the ways in which soldiers found mutual support as they confronted an uncertain and perilous future. Similarly, training not only prepared the conscripts for battle, but it also provided routine: recruits were kept busy with drill, firing practice, and sentry duty. Commanding officers well knew that one of the forces most corrosive to morale was boredom and listlessness. Through a multitude of such ways, both consciously and incidentally, all units in every army fostered an *esprit de corps*.

Discipline was considered essential not only to ensure combat effectiveness, but to give a soldier's life order and direction after the shock of conscription. It could be brutal. Russian soldiers were subjected to regular beatings, since obedience was believed by most officers to be the key to success on the battlefield. Any soldier who ducked an oncoming cannonball would be whipped, for (it was argued) such attempts to dodge a shell only encouraged the enemy. A soldier deemed guilty of 'cowardice' could be shot immediately. One of the severest of Prussian punishments was 'running the gauntlet' (forcing a soldier to pass between two lines of whip-wielding soldiers). The French, who had abolished flogging as unworthy of the citizen-soldier in 1789, nonetheless retained a draconian disciplinary code in every other sense. Military justice was prompt, inflexible, and severe: the *boulet* involved confinement with a ball and chain, while the death penalty was passed by courts martial for a wide array of offences, from minor acts of pillage to cowardice in battle. In the British army, punishments ranged from short spells of imprisonment, flogging, 'running the gauntlet', 'riding the wooden horse' (sitting astride the sharp apex of a triangular box), and death by shooting or hanging.

Yet in every major belligerent, there were voices which urged that a change was needed in discipline, which should emphasize, first and foremost, appeals to a soldier's honour, *esprit de corps*, patriotism, leadership, and mutual respect between officers and men. In the French army, two decades of revolution and war had ingrained these values anyway. As citizen-soldiers, French conscripts enjoyed a status other than as pariahs: under the Republic, they were fêted as *défenseurs de la patrie*, defenders of the fatherland. Napoleon honoured bravery and merit, regardless of rank, with the *Légion d'Honneur*. In one incident in 1814, a French captain struck one of his men with the flat of his sabre, but the furious cavalryman spun on the officer, showed him his *Légion d'Honneur* and shamed his superior into an apology. The two men shook hands and later shared their rations and a bottle of brandy.

The Russian War Minister, General Barclay de Tolly, admonished his officers to treat their soldiers with more humanity: 'The Russian soldier has all the highest military virtues: he is brave, zealous, obedient, devoted, and not wayward; consequently there are certainly ways, without employing cruelty, to train him and to maintain discipline.' Amongst the British redcoats, short spells of imprisonment and small fines began to replace flogging for some offences. Even in iron-hard Prussia, the military reformer August von Gneisenau proclaimed the 'freedom of the backs' when he reduced the use of flogging.

Esprit de corps and discipline were ultimately geared to ensure the army's cohesion and effectiveness when campaigning began. Yet there were some factors that even the best-trained armies struggled with. Long marches in extreme conditions could break down discipline. In its lightning strike against Austria in 1805, the *Grande Armée* marched 300 miles in thirteen days, but prior to that, most of the army (which had been poised to invade Britain) had to cross France by forced marches. The footsoldier (later captain) Jean-Roch Coignet described marching day and night with less than an hour of sleep, so that the exhausted men locked arms to prevent themselves from falling over. Coignet eventually succumbed to fatigue and tumbled into a ditch. The remarkable achievement was that the French were still able to land such a fast series of devastating blows at the end of it all. The effects were very different seven years later, during the long march into Russia, when the distances were so vast, the summer heat so stifling, and opportunities for foraging so sparse that men collapsed and deserted. The commander of the Bavarian contingent in Napoleon's invading army reported that the agonies of the march brought about 'such a widespread spirit of depression, discouragement, discontent, disobedience, and insubordination that one cannot forecast what will happen'. What happened was that troops deserted in droves: the entire army may have lost as much as a third of its strength by the time it had reached Vitebsk, scarcely halfway to Moscow.

The other enemy was disease: more men died from sickness in the French Wars than from enemy action. In the Peninsular War, the British lost 24,930 men to illness, compared with 8,889 to French fire, a pattern repeated across Europe wherever men were encamped, barracked, or bivouacked in close quarters. Archaeological evidence uncovered from mass graves in Vilnius in 2001 suggests that close to a third of the French troops on the retreat from Moscow in 1812 were afflicted with typhus-carrying lice. Another horror was venereal disease: the very reputation of European soldiery for violence and coarseness meant that, while men having romances with local women was not unknown, most turned to prostitutes in their desperate need for sexual pleasure. The result, as one French cavalryman put it, was that the hospitals were 'piled high with the victims of a depraved love'.

Soldiers who survived battle, but who were captured, experienced varying fates according to when and by whom they were held as prisoners of war. During the first years of the French Revolutionary Wars, allied captives taken by the French were held in towns and citadels, paid according to their rank, and allowed to roam freely around town, provided they submitted to the daily roll calls and gave their word of honour that they would not abscond. Marriage between PoWs and local women was not uncommon, and many took up the trades they had pursued in civilian life. Conditions became harsher during the Terror, involving confinement, but were relaxed again afterwards, partly for pragmatic reasons, since many French communes simply did not have the resources to keep prisoners under lock and key indeterminately. Prisoners taken by the British were held in fortresses around the country (including, famously, Edinburgh Castle). Conditions for incarcerated PoWs could be pestilential. A French conscript in 1799 who spent nine months in Austrian captivity emerged 'sick and gnawed by vermin', confined 'forty men to a room', with no fresh air, poor food, and a pile of rotten straw as a bed. He was exposed to reprisals from the local peasants, who spat at, beat, and punched the French prisoners when they were allowed to watch a religious procession. This particular conscript was fortunately released thanks to an exchange of prisoners. Such exchanges often occurred for political reasons: the discussions were used as a means of sounding out one's opponents for peace negotiations.

The full horrors of war were unleashed on the battlefield. While armies in the French Wars did little to innovate in terms of new weaponry (although the British experimented, not altogether successfully, with rockets), their tools of death were devastating enough. Across both sides, the total number killed and wounded at Austerlitz was 24,000, at Jena-Auerstadt, 60,000, at Eylau, 56,000, at Waterloo, 46,000. The worst bloodletting was at Borodino, where 80,000 were killed (and 35,000 wounded on the French side alone, of whom 13,000 later died). These were battles each fought in a single day, a slaughter on a scale equal to that of the First World War: the British took 58,000 casualties on the first day of the Somme in 1916.

During the French Wars, although a musket took no less than twelve steps to load and fire, a well-trained soldier could discharge four rounds in three minutes, unleashing a rapid series of volleys which, according to the lists of wounds treated by the French medical service, spared no part of the human body, from the cranium to the toes. A heavy cavalry sabre could slice through a man's hat and then cleave his head in two. The impact of artillery was so horrifying that even battle-hardened surgeons were unsettled by some of the sights: a gunner killed instantly when a cannonball smashed through his rib-cage, or an officer decapitated by a shell, his headless torso still wedged in the saddle.

Soldiers' memoirs also record the carnage of battle: at Aspern-Essling in 1809, Coignet was hurled off his feet by a cannonball which ripped through a line of men nearby. 'I could no longer feel my right arm. Looking down, I saw a bloody scrap hanging over the bleeding wound, as if my arm had been shattered. It was actually one of the remains of my poor comrades which had been thrown all over me.' In the aftermath, every battlefield presented such a sight, sound, and smell of death that it seared itself onto the memory of those who experienced it. After Eylau, a French soldier later described the wintry field where 'everywhere, large trails of blood coloured the snow, turning yellow with the trampling of men and horses. The sites of cavalry charges, bayonet attacks and gun emplacements were covered with dead men and horses. Wherever you looked, you saw nothing but corpses, or wretches who were dragging themselves away, you could hear only piercing cries.' The wounded were treated by surgeons who coped as best they could with the scale and number of casualties, but the worst wounds were dealt with by amputation. A skilled surgeon could saw off a limb in a matter of minutes: the French surgeon Dominique Larrey is said to have performed 200 during the appalling carnage at Borodino. Larrey was in fact a great innovator: in 1794, he created 'flying ambulances', specially designed carts to bring help to the wounded who could not be carried from the battlefield to the dressing stations in the rear and to evacuate those who could. Later, he devised the first system of triage, categorizing wounds according to severity and then allocating different levels of care to the men in each. In 1796, he told his staff to treat the most severely wounded first, regardless of their rank and nationality. Such was his reputation that, when Wellington spotted Larrey's ambulances at work at Waterloo, he took of his hat, telling one of his officers that 'I salute the courage and devotion of an age that is no longer ours'.

The civilian's war

The war affected civilians in a multitude of ways. Few were mad enough to behave like Pierre Bezukhov, Tolstoy's character from *War and Peace* who blundered around the killing fields of

Borodino, but they were more likely to be caught in the cross-fire, particularly when the battle took place in or near a town. As the coalition forces closed in on the French in Leipzig in 1813, they shelled the surrounding villages, an experience recalled by a Saxon pastor who described the panic as people sheltered in cellars. Some took refuge in the church, but shot blasted out the doors and fell through the windows, and the tower caught light. Some civilians attached themselves to the army, however: Orthodox priests were known to stand in Russian firing lines to encourage the soldiers. More usually, there were civilians in the rear who supported the armies in different ways—and they were often women. In the French army, there were the *cantinières* and *vivandières*, women who had followed husbands or lovers on campaign and sold food and provisions to get by. Often clad in spare parts of uniforms and sharing the hardships of life on the march, they were formidable, but popular, figures amongst the soldiers. On the retreat from Moscow, the French sergeant Bourgogne recalled the stoicism of 'our *cantinière*, Madame Dubois', who was married to the regimental surgeon. She gave birth in the forest, in sub-zero temperatures. The next day, the colonel gave the mother his horse and she carried her new born baby wrapped in a sheepskin. The British army, too, had its 'regimental women', wives of soldiers who, as one Scot said of his spouse, 'shared with me all my fortunes over field and flood, in camp and in quarters, in war and in peace, without any unpleasant reflection at her own share of the suffering'. This particular couple married in the field and spent their wedding night in a tent shared with eleven other men.

On rare occasions, women saw combat: Thérèse Figueur fought as a dragoon with the French army from 1793 until she was captured outside Burgos in Spain by the guerrilla leader Merino in 1812. She spent the rest of the war in captivity in Britain. Estimates of the numbers of such French female soldiers range from 30 to 80. Women could be found on some French naval vessels, usually as cooks: at Trafalgar, the crew of HMS *Revenge* rescued a 25-year-old

Frenchwoman who had leaped into the sea to escape the *Achille*, which had burned and exploded during the battle. More usually, however, civilians were victims in the destructive path of the war. Women were all too often subjected to sexual assault: the crime was endemic enough to prompt Napoleon to admonish his men on the eve of their landing in Egypt in 1798 that 'in all countries, one thing is universal: rape is a monstrosity'. But not all soldiers listened. When an invading army 'lived off the land' and plundered, a family faced not only destitution, but violence. In the Rhineland in 1795, a French officer frankly admitted that 'there was murder, rape, looting of every kind—everything possible was committed. I saw the wretched schoolmaster at Anternheim (who had six young children) murdered in his own home, as well as the pastor at Albig and a number of other unfortunate victims. Their only offence was not to give up promptly enough what little money they might have had.'

8. The steep climb, the fallen—and falling—bodies and the close quarters of the fighting illustrate the terror and exhaustion of siege warfare

Particularly horrifying was the experience of the populace of a city taken by storm. Soldiers forced to battle their way through a 'forlorn hope'—a breach in fortifications blasted by artillery—were subjected to an exhausting ordeal and a terrifying gauntlet of fire (see Figure 8). Once the city was captured, officers lost all control of their men: when the British took the Spanish town of Badajoz in 1812 after sustaining horrifying casualties, the men ran amok, a shocked lieutenant reporting that he had been horrified to see men 'turn upon the already too deeply injured females, and tear from them trinkets that adorned their necks, fingers and ears! And finally they would strip them of their wearing apparel... many men were flogged, but... none were hanged—yet hundreds deserved it.' Unsurprisingly, the approach of an invading army provoked a flight of refugees. In Germany in 1813, a journalist living in Leipzig described 'Weeping mothers with featherbeds packed into baskets, two or three nearly naked children in tow, their infants on their backs; fathers looking for their wives and children; children who had lost their parents in the crowd; sick people in wheelbarrows being pushed through the throng of horses; everywhere weeping and lamentation.'

Chapter 6
The war at sea

After Nelson's utter destruction of the French fleet at Aboukir in 1798, Bonaparte wrote that 'the fates seem to have decided to prove to us that, if they have granted us hegemony on land, they have made our rivals the rulers of the waves'. This was partly because the Royal Navy was by far the largest of any in the eighteenth century: in 1795, the British fleet had 123 ships of the line as against the next largest, the French, which could muster 56 (already down from 73 at the outbreak of war). Nonetheless, size alone could not account for the success of the British navy at securing maritime dominance: when the French had other maritime powers like the Spanish (76 ships of the line) and the Dutch (28) as allies (as they did at various stages during the wars), they could potentially stretch the Royal Navy's capacity to breaking point, since its responsibilities included the defence of home waters, keeping watch on enemy fleets in European seas, the protection of sea lanes and of the empire, and their use in amphibious ('combined') operations.

So quality also counted, particularly in Britain's sailors, for the very scale of the navy's commitments ensured that even the rawest of recruits soon tasted life at sea. From 1793, the navy blockaded the French coast, giving the British crews a wide experience of sailing a vessel in all kinds of weather and seas. British ships may have been more sluggish than their sleeker French or Spanish counterparts, but what they lacked in speed was more than compensated for by the skill of their crews in handling a vessel in the most difficult of conditions. In combat, the ability of a British crew to steer their ship close to the enemy allowed them to make use of their superior gunnery, since they also had more experience of firing at sea. The role of the Royal Navy in cooperating with the army in combined operations is often neglected. During the Seven Years War, the Admiralty had approved a design for a flat-bottomed landing craft which remained the basic vessel for such operations. The most dramatic during the Napoleonic Wars was undoubtedly the withdrawal of General Sir John Moore's army from the Spanish port of La Coruña in January 1809. Naval support was also one of the essential ingredients for ultimate allied success in the Peninsular War. The very survival of Wellington's army when lodged behind the lines of Torres Vedras around Lisbon was dependent upon the Royal Navy's ability to feed and supply the 420,000 soldiers and civilians by transporting grain from North America, cattle from North Africa, and saltpetre from Bengal. Between 1808 and 1813, the navy kept up a steady flow of muskets, pistols, cartridges, and artillery pieces to arm not just the regular forces, but also the Spanish guerrillas. Wellington acknowledged the role of the navy when he commented that 'our maritime superiority gives me the power of maintaining my army while the enemy are unable to do so'.

The main problems confronting the British were twofold: the Royal Navy faced persistent difficulties of manning its vessels and there was the wear and tear of relentless campaigning at sea. The latter arose mainly because of one of the navy's greatest, if unglamorous, achievements: the dogged blockade of the French coast, which took its toll in wrecks and damages. By Trafalgar only 83 out of 136 ships of the line were fit for service: 'I wish we had peace', lamented William Marsden, Secretary to the Admiralty in January 1805, 'and could lay our ships up in dock. They are worn out like post-horses during a general election.' The government responded with an intensive programme of shipbuilding, but numbers were also made up by prizes—which always accounted for at least a quarter of the navy's strength. Within four years, the navy had 113 seaworthy ships of the line, to which were added the 596 cruisers, which had trebled in number since 1793, as the navy used every sinew to prosecute the war: it was the only time in history before the Second World War that one navy deployed half of the world's warships (the US Navy outstripped that achievement in 1945).

The navy's shortages of manpower arose because men were understandably reluctant to serve out of self-preservation, a natural aversion to iron discipline, and the higher rates of pay offered by merchantmen and privateers. Wartime absences from home and even from *any land at all* could last for a very long time, since a ship might be at sea for months—even years—without putting into port. Still, perhaps two-thirds of sailors were volunteers, including deserters from European navies and blacks, some of whom had escaped from slavery. Volunteers were drawn by the promise of prize money for the capture of an enemy ship, although the lion's share went to the officers. While criminals were never accepted as recruits, joining the navy was one way for debtors to get out of prison, since the Admiralty paid off the money which they owed, provided it came to no more than £20. Yet there were never enough volunteers, so the Impress Service was created in 1793 to use varying degrees of 'persuasion' in Britain's ports: it was certainly unjust, but it ensured that the ships of the Royal Navy were well (if not always fully) manned. Parties from ships of the line would seize sailors from in-bound merchant vessels, while on shore an officer would establish his headquarters (usually in a tavern), where volunteers would be accommodated and the less fortunate souls who had been press-ganged would be locked up. Small, auxiliary vessels called tenders would sit in the harbour to transport the recruits to the naval bases at Portsmouth, Plymouth, and the Nore. Meanwhile gangs of sailors, who were paid incentives for every man recruited, were sent out to persuade, cajole, and force men into the King's service. Those who were pressed were usually people with seafaring skills—often they were sailors already, for the bounty was higher for a seaman than for a landlubber. Violence was actually rare, but the arrival of a press gang in a port was certainly a time to draw breath: the magistrates, with an anxious eye on public order, did their best to frustrate the recruiting parties—even to the point of throwing the officers in the clink. The gangs tended to fall on the least influential people in society, but they provoked local hostility nonetheless. William Henry Dillon, a lieutenant in the Impress Service, commented on his soul-destroying work in Hull in 1803:

> In this performing my unpleasant duties, I soon experienced the ill will of the mob. On one occasion I was assaulted by a shower of brickbats: on another, a volley of either musket or pistol balls was fired into my room one evening as I was reading at my table.

Such opposition, paradoxically, existed alongside support for the war itself—it was just that, understandably, people did not want to have to leave their homes and jobs, nor lose valued members of their communities, to fight it. Magistrates did sometimes see the arrival of the Impress Service as an opportunity to get rid of paupers and petty criminals, but the difficulty then was in persuading the gangs to accept them.

One has good cause to suppose that in such an isolated world as a warship at sea, such a rag-bag collection of often reluctant men could only be forced into performing the arduous, muscular work of sailing a wooden ship and of standing firm in battle by the lash. Yet the image of an eighteenth-century naval vessel as 'a sort of floating concentration camp' has been overdrawn. Instead, the British navy was a reflection of British society: it was governed by a hierarchy that ruled through a mixture of repression, concessions, moral control, and acquiescence 'from below'. Some historians—and there are dissenting voices—have argued that British society had a 'disordered cohesion' and this, the naval historian Nicholas Rodger suggests, is a term which aptly describes the navy itself. Naval life was, by the orderly standards of a modern fleet, chaotic, but what kept the men in line was less the brutality of discipline than a strong sense of common purpose with their officers and an awareness of the dangers which awaited them. In such circumstances, a brutal officer was a weak and inefficient officer, since he could only command obedience through violence.

In any case, imposing the harsher punishments was difficult: according to the regulations (the Articles of War), a captain could only impose a maximum sentence of a flogging with twelve lashes. Anything more required the time-consuming and unpredictable process of a court martial—and such tribunals proved remarkably reluctant to convict. A court martial could impose the death penalty for twenty offences (including desertion and striking an officer), but this was actually milder than the sanguinary justice meted out to British civilians on shore, who could find themselves dangling from the gallows for no less than 200 types of crime. Naval courts martial tended to impose death sentences on two offences only—murder and (probably reflecting religious scruples) buggery—although the alternative sentences (of several hundred lashes, for example) could scarcely be described as a light alternative. In general, however, a ship's captain depended more on the men's conviction that obedience was the best way to ensure survival, rather than on a persistent use of force. A ship could not function if the men were reduced to unthinking beasts of burden ruled by the lash: fighting at sea demanded a great deal of personal initiative. Perhaps a model commander in terms of his approach to discipline was a Captain Twisden of the British frigate *Révolutionnaire* in 1801:

> His ship was a pattern of order and discipline, and splendidly manned; and of both ship and crew he was justly proud....Captain Twisden did not punish as often, or as severely, as I have known some far less efficient officers to do; but his discipline was regular and systematic, never acted upon by whim or caprice.

If French army officers were noted for their aggression, courage, and initiative, they had their maritime counterparts in the British navy. Confidence in their ships and their men bred a fiery and determined brand of command in the Royal Navy, which relied heavily on the personal initiative of individual commanders. On the eve of Trafalgar, Nelson's orders to his officers made it crystal clear that, in the smoke and confusion of battle, in which signals from his flagship would be obscured, he relied upon his captains to seize the opportunities as they arose: 'No captain can do very wrong if he places his ship alongside that of an enemy.'

The French and Spanish navies

Like the Royal Navy, the French and Spanish suffered from structural problems, but found them harder to overcome. The former were starved of manpower and naval supplies. France lacked the materials needed to replace serious losses at sea and, with the British blockade, supplies of timber, rigging, and sails from the Black Sea and the Baltic dried up. The monarchy had stockpiled vast stores of timber, rope, and other supplies, but the entire store for the Mediterranean fleet at Toulon was incinerated when the British took the port in 1793, burned down the naval arsenal, and towed off thirteen ships of the line. By 1795, French shipbuilders no longer had enough timber to construct larger vessels. In 1805, even with their own problems, the British outnumbered the combined French and Spanish navies by two to one. Meanwhile, despite the size of the French population, the numbers of those 'following the sea' were small, not least because in what was still primarily an agricultural economy, the usual nurseries of naval seamen—deep-sea fishing and commercial shipping—were relatively small. In all, it has been estimated that France had a reserve of no more than 60,000 trained sailors by 1789. Both the old regime and the Revolution therefore suffered from chronic manpower shortages. Recruitment was systematic, but overstretched: the French had tens of ships, but not enough men to sail them properly. All men in maritime towns and villages had to register on rolls which were divided into 'classes'. Every three to five years, each 'class' was obliged to serve a year at sea. In theory, this would provide the navy with a trained reserve, but in practice this deeply resented form of recruitment had little effect because men found ways to avoid it. The Revolution retained this system, so did little to address the underlying problem. During the Terror of 1793–4, all sailors and maritime workers were made liable to conscription, but such measures could only go so far in providing the navy with skilled sailors. The effectiveness of the British blockade was such that, while the British could train their recruits 'on the job' on the high seas, a French squadron which sortied from Brest in July 1795 consisted of crews two-thirds of whom had never been to sea before. In such circumstances, the losses of the experienced men in battle (at a rate of 10 per cent at the 'Glorious First of June' in 1794 and the Battle of Aboukir in 1798) were disastrous.

Apart from a paucity of skill and practice, French and Spanish crews also had little experience of gunnery at sea, which was combined with a technical difference from their British opponents. While British guns were fired with flintlocks, both French and Spanish navies used slow-burning matches. The precise moment of firing was therefore unpredictable and so aiming a cannon from a ship rolling in the ocean swell was impossible. Above all, French gunners had what some French commanders were beginning to regard as the bad habit of firing not at the hulls of the enemy ships, but at the rigging in order to disable them. The instinct to do so may have come from the fact that the more experienced men in the French navy were frequently recruited from privateers. When chased by enemy ships, French privateers would usually blast at the enemy's masts and rigging in the hope of slowing down their pursuers. Some French captains tried to break this habit, which wasted hundreds of shots, but with little success. A story circulated that when a French shell actually smashed into the hull of an enemy vessel, the stunned British crew recovered from the shock when a sailor stood exposed in the ragged gash in the ship's side, joking, 'My God, I'll be safest here, because they'll never be able to fire two shots through the same hole!' The British always fired at the hull, because it could kill off and demoralize enemy gunners. It also left the masts and rigging intact so that, when the ship was captured, it could be sailed off as a prize. Moreover, by aiming low, a British gun was more likely to hit *something*, rather than see the shot whistle harmlessly past the enemy's masts and rigging.

In addition to these problems, the French Revolution has often been blamed for breaking down discipline, while also destroying the experienced officer corps inherited from the Bourbon monarchy. It is certainly true that the early years of the French Revolution were accompanied by a wave of mutinies and insubordination which, by 1791, drove away much of the demoralized officer corps of the royal navy. In October that year, 47 per cent of officers based in Brest, home of the French Atlantic fleet, were absent without leave. By the outbreak of the war in 1792, there remained only 42 of 170 captains. This dissolution of the French officer corps seriously undermined the navy just as the French Republic was about to go head to head against the maritime might of Great Britain. The Revolution had responded to the crisis in April 1791 by opening naval commissions to any seaman with five years of experience at sea, which was aimed primarily at drawing in officers from the merchant marine. Naval historians have subsequently claimed that the admission of civilian sailors was a blow to the professionalism of the French navy. Yet it is important not to overstate the damage caused in the long run. The *upper* ranks of the professional officer corps may have been severely thinned by flight and absenteeism, but of 530 lieutenants in the old navy, 356 remained at their posts and rose rapidly during the decade or so before Trafalgar. The leading French protagonists during the campaign of 1805—Villeneuve, Rosily, Decrès, Missiessy—had all been lieutenants in 1789. While it is true that the commercial seamen drawn into the officer corps had no experience of sailing the heavier naval vessels, if given the chance to train they might have learned to do so. Yet they never did get that opportunity, because from 1793, the French coast was blockaded by the Royal Navy.

In August 1790, the National Assembly introduced a penal code for the navy, trying to relax some of the harsher punishments of minor infractions, while maintaining the discipline necessary for a military vessel. Punishments were formally calibrated according to the offence, removing some of the arbitrary power which captains had exercised over their crews. For some breaches of discipline, sailors were to be tried by a jury of their peers. Other cases were to be heard by courts martial. Nonetheless, some of the harshest penalties were retained, including flogging (which was abolished in the army in 1789), running the gauntlet, and the *cale*, by which the victim would be tied to a line lashed to the end of the yardarm, from which he would be repeatedly plunged into the water below. Punishments even for small transgressions could still include being tied to a mast or shackled in leg irons. Some French sailors had clearly expected a more radical overhaul of naval justice and their frustration was expressed in a mutiny in the roadstead off Brest that September. The target of the sailors' ire was the harsher punishments, particularly those which they considered humiliating: the leg irons weighed down by trailing chains, for example, were likened to the chains worn by convicts who served in the penal galleys at Brest. The Assembly reacted to the mutiny by amending the Code, expunging some of the harsher punishments. Nonetheless, interference from the local authorities and from political clubs on shore continued to undermine the obedience of the sailors.

During the Terror, there was a concerted effort to restore discipline. Counter-revolution amongst the officers and the more intransigent breaches of discipline among the men were punished with death. In January 1794, for example, four mutineers had their heads sliced off by a guillotine erected on a pontoon in the roadstead of Brest, in front of the assembled fleet. The government's naval expert, Jeanbon Saint-André, imposed a new penal code, which reserved the harshest of sanctions for defiance or disobedience, including being clapped in irons, flogged, imprisoned, or guillotined. The revolutionary government also sought to galvanize the sailors with patriotic fervour.

Discipline and motivation were all very well, but that had to be supported with material supplies. The provision of the scarce resources necessary for the navy could only continue if the Terror itself continued, with the economic controls associated with it. This was because the French economy of the mid-1790s was already struggling to meet the demands of the war on the continent. In 1793–4, the needs of *both* French maritime *and* territorial power could only be met from the threadbare French economy through coercion, that is, by terrorizing the population. Yet the Thermidorians (the republicans who toppled the Jacobins and ended the Terror in July 1794) were in no mood to continue with the draconian measures associated with the revolutionary dictatorship. They may inadvertently have prevented the Republic from building the revolutionary navy which was in the making.

The conflicting pressures of the war point to another major headache for the French—and it was perhaps the main reason why, for all the resources at its disposal, France was never able to obtain parity with the British. Geography ensured that, unlike Britain, France was 'amphibious', meaning a continental as well as a maritime state. The political desire to sustain both commitments was always there, but the wherewithal to do so was not. During the Revolutionary and Napoleonic Wars, the ravenous demands of the French war effort for men, money, and material could be met through exploiting the conquests in western and southern Europe, but this was of little use to the navy, since the territories conquered were not good sources of naval supplies, which came from the Baltic and the Black Sea. In any case, the expansionism which this involved, especially under Napoleon, committed France deeper and deeper to the continental war, as the great European powers, with British support, sought to cut France down to size. Despite the resources and political ingenuity at its disposal, France could be either a maritime or a territorial power. It could not be both.

The Spanish fleet suffered from similar structural problems. For one, despite its long coastlines, it faced a perennial shortage of manpower. In a system established in 1737, anyone who worked as a sailor or shipwright, even in such civilian activities as deep-sea fishing and ocean-going commerce, had to register on a list (*matricula del mar*) so that they could be called up in time of war, in return for which they were exempt from army conscription. By the French Wars, the numbers registered seemed to have hit a ceiling, at 65,000, which was not enough to man the Spanish navy, since the government's own estimates required 110,000 men—and not all of those registered could be recruited as Spain still needed its fishermen, merchant sailors, and shipbuilders. Worse, the number of registrants dropped with the outbreak of war, while those who were already on the lists deserted in a flood: by 1808, the numbers on the register had shrivelled to 41,000 men.

The shortfall was made up of people who were semi-trained (if there had been time to train them) and some of whom had no experience of sailing at all: impoverished shepherds and landless peasants from such places as Castille and Extremadura. While British gunners needed 90 seconds to load, fire, sponge out, and reload a 32-pounder, their Spanish counterparts took five minutes. The captain of the *Conde de Regla* complained that of a crew of 500, no more than 60 had experience of the high seas, the rest being coastal fishermen or sailors 'without training or any understanding whatsoever of a ship's rigging or routine on board'—and there was no time to teach them. The situation was made desperate on the very eve of Trafalgar because yellow fever ravaged Spain's ports, which decimated an already thinly spread pool of recruits.

There was also a shortage of naval stores: while the forests of the Asturias could supply most of the oak for Spanish hulls, Spain had serious difficulty in securing resin, tar, pitch, rope, and iron, which had to be imported from Russia and Sweden, supplies which were choked off by the British blockade while Spain was allied to France between 1796 and 1808, with only a brief period of peace in 1802–3. The situation was not this grim all the time: when they did have access to their empire, the Spanish built fine vessels. The colonial port of Havana produced some of the mightiest ships of line in the world, made from durable tropical wood like mahogany and teak, rather than European oak and beech: the *Santisima Trinidad,* captured by the British at Trafalgar and sunk in the storm which followed, was the largest vessel of the age. Yet, for all its virtues, the Spanish fleet was neither big enough, nor adequately manned to meet its long list of commitments, which included defending Spain's overseas empire in the Americas and the Pacific, protecting its trade routes, and fighting the war in European waters.

Combat

Naval combat strained every human nerve to the limits of its endurance. The physical danger was desperately close: a single broadside from an eighteenth-century three-deck warship would send a half ton of metal into the hull of an enemy ship (see Figure 9). At point-blank range in the close quarters of naval combat, this was devastating. Cannon balls, jagged wooden splinters, and fragments of iron from canister shot spun on unpredictable trajectories through the cramped spaces in the gun decks. The metal shot might ricochet between the decks before finally being spent: it did not have to strike a man to kill him, since the shock alone of a near miss would do the same. The concussion of cannon was deafening: in some close engagements, men lost their hearing for life, though they tried to protect their ears by binding rags around their head. And all this was experienced in near-darkness on the gun decks, where, according

9. This nineteenth-century lithograph captures the awe-inspiring power of a ship of the line

to one British writer, it was 'as if all the tenants of the lower regions, black from smoke, had broken loose and gone mad'. The feeble light let in by the gun ports was obscured by the barrels of the cannon—and, at close range, the hull of the enemy ship. The interior was filled with the sulphurous smoke from the gunfire and sometimes from burning wood and sail. The momentary light from muzzle flashes compounded the vision of hell. Outside, the atmosphere was equally outlandish. 'Bursting forth from the many black iron mouths, and whirling rapidly in thick rings, till it swells into hills and mountains, through which the sharp red tongue of death darts flash after flash, and mingling fire, the smoke rolls upward like a curtain, in awful beauty.' Before the killing and the maiming relented, the dead and wounded lay amongst the wreckage of gun carriages, trapped beneath fallen debris and, on the exposed quarter decks, pinned down by fallen masts, or tangled in shredded rigging and sails. The surgeon's post was a scene of agony and butchery as limbs were amputated and blood seeped across the decks. 'And ever and anon, amid the breaks of the cannon's peal, the shrieks and cries of the wounded mingled with the deep roar of the outpoured and constantly-reiterated "hurra! hurra! hurra!" A chorus of cataracts sweep over the rippled smiles of the patient, passionless, and unconscious sea. Sulphur and fire, agony, death and horror, are riding and revelling on its bosom.'

Chapter 7
The people's war

The fighting on land and sea were the furnaces in which the full horrors of war were felt and the scale of the conflict foreshadowed the terrible sufferings in the 'total wars' of the twentieth century. So, too, did the attempts by the belligerents to mobilize their peoples for the struggle. The French, as we have seen, made strenuous efforts to do so, but so did their enemies. In 1812, Clausewitz opined that now 'it is not the king who wages war on the king, not an army against another army, but a people against another people'. Governments, churches, intellectuals, the press, and cultural organizations tried different ways of rousing the people to fight, but, as many old regime politicians saw, there were dangers in rousing the masses. Some officials argued that the only way to survive the Napoleonic onslaught was by adopting some of the reforms of the very Revolution that they were fighting against. As the Prussian reformer Gneisenau put it, 'the Revolution has set into motion the entire French people on an equal social and political basis, thereby abolishing the former balance of power. If the other states wish to re-establish this balance, they must use the same resources.' That, he added, meant borrowing from 'the arsenal of the Revolution'.

Yet, while *all* the major belligerents did implement reforms, it was to wildly varying degrees and in most cases their fundamental social and political structures remained unchanged: even the military was only tinkered with rather than overhauled. Most European politicians had no desire to alter the old order beyond recognition, let alone to abandon absolute monarchy. Some of their inspiration for change pre-dated the wars, flowing from the heritage of 'enlightened absolutism' prior to 1789. Governments were also confronted by privileged interests, such as the nobles and the Church, who were often powerful enough to obstruct reform. The most radical programme arose in Prussia, partly in response to the humiliating disaster at Jena in 1806, but also because it reconnected with a tradition of enlightened reform from the days of Frederick the Great.

Yet, while Prussia's contribution to the ultimate allied victory was very important, the military efforts of determinedly conservative Austria and Russia were equally weighty, perhaps decisively so. After 1812, Russia's contribution to the defeat of Napoleon in terms of persistence, commitment of troops, and diplomatic leadership almost outdid all the individual efforts of its allies: only Austria fielded a larger army in late 1813–14. What this suggests is that Napoleon was eventually defeated not, primarily, with the help of root-and-branch reform, but by old regime states which had remained fundamentally unchanged. This also raises the question as to how far patriotic fervour was a factor in the final victory of the allies.

Nationalism, loosely defined here as a sense of loyalty to a particular people with its own sense of ethnic or political identity, accompanied by a belief that this nation should be as united and as independent as possible, was certainly expressed in response to Napoleon in these years, but it was usually uttered by intellectuals who often did not intend their thoughts to be for popular consumption. The Berlin lectures of Johann Gottlieb Fichte in the winter of 1807–8, for example, are often taken to be a great trumpet call for German nationalism, but he was addressing himself to Prussia's intellectual cream, 'the foremost and immediate embodiments of precious national qualities'. The unwashed masses would only become part of the 'people' (*Volk*) after a long process of national education. With some notable exceptions, the European elites were generally wary about mobilizing the people, since the outcome for the old order was unpredictable. Recent historians have also become more cautious about stressing nationalism as a motivation amongst the people themselves. In researching what the people were being *urged* to fight for and what *they thought* they were fighting for, they have found that, almost everywhere, the war sharpened identities, but this rarely translated into a resistance driven by full-blown aspirations for national unity and independence. Rather, they were focused on older pieties, on Church, King, province, or town. For contemporaries, the example of Spanish resistance after 1808 showed what a popular uprising could do against the French, but at the same time it confirmed prejudices about the destructive capacities of 'the mob'.

Spain

The Spanish struggle against Napoleon in 1808–14 is remembered as the 'War of Independence', which suggests a fight for national freedom from French domination. That was certainly how the Peninsular War ended and there was some political direction to the uprising, in the shape of the Spanish parliament, the Cortes, which was convoked in 1810 by the provincial juntas and elected on a broad suffrage. Meeting in Cadiz, the Cortes passed a series of laws which attacked the old regime in Spain, including the freedom of the press and the abolition of the Inquisition (by then primarily a system of censorship). This reform culminated in the Constitution of 1812 which created a constitutional monarchy, with the ringing declaration in its first three articles that 'the Spanish nation is free and independent... Power resides essentially in the nation.' Yet if it was one thing for a parliament to try to give the struggle liberal leadership, it was quite another for the people as a whole to take notice. Recent research on the guerrilla war has relentlessly stripped away the myths, created when the more famous guerrilla leaders, such as Juan Martín Diez—'El Empecinado', the Stubborn One—emerged as victors in 1814 and explained their motives as a fiery combination of revenge, honour, and patriotism.

While it is unlikely that the guerrillas shared the vision proffered by the liberals in the Cortes, they also seem to have been indifferent to the Church and the King: many bands actually survived by plundering the former. Most guerrilla leaders fought to enrich and aggrandize themselves, which may explain why they were so resistant to political direction from Cadiz. Those who did effectively ceased to become guerrillas and were absorbed by the regular forces, which was not a popular option amongst the guerrilla rank and file. The historian Michael Broers has shown that, while many guerrilla leaders sought recognition, legitimacy, and respectability by demanding official commissions from the Cortes, the most successful in recruiting ever-larger numbers were those who had the most success in looting and plunder.

At the very most, many guerrillas felt that they were fighting for their provinces (outside of which they did not serve) and their villages, rather than for Spain. Even then, research by the historian Charles Esdaile has shown that the guerrillas were not averse to plundering their own communities—that they were, in effect, bandits and little more (see Figure 10). The war certainly offered rich if dangerous pickings from brigandage. Not all guerrillas were *originally* engaged in criminality: they may have been driven into open revolt by French brutality, whereupon seizing the spoils became part of their culture, a means even of survival, but was not part of the initial motivation. Perhaps what bound together a range of guerrilla leaders—whatever their motivations—was, as Broers suggests, 'a shared culture, that of honour and vendetta, that gave rise to a certain style of leadership', but it was also characterized by a collective denial that they visited the same horrors on Spaniards as they did on the French.

10. Goya's etching depicts the brutally ambiguous motivations of the Spanish guerrillas

Historians have also questioned the effectiveness of the guerrillas in helping the British–Portuguese forces under Wellington defeat the French. While they may have caused as many as 180,000 French casualties, tied down French forces, provided intelligence to the allies, and discouraged collaboration, it has been pointed out that they could never prevent the French from concentrating their armies against the allies when they needed to. 'The guerrillas', wrote Wellington after a close inspection, 'although active and willing, and although their operations in general occasion the utmost annoyance to the enemy, are so little disciplined that they can do nothing against the French troops unless the latter are very inferior in numbers.'

French evidence, however, suggests that they were more than an annoyance. As the historian John Tone has suggested, the ghastly cycle of atrocities and vengeance on both sides meant that, whether or not the fighters were 'heroes' or 'villains', the regular systems of French civil rule—the gendarmerie, the civilian administration, the law courts—could never function properly, if they did at all, while the French army never enjoyed a stable, core base in Spain from which to launch their operations against the regular allied forces. If the guerrilla struggle was neither a war of national liberation, nor a struggle for Church and King, for the French it was an exhausting war nevertheless.

Prussia and Austria

The Prussian experience was quite different. The purpose of the prime movers of Prussian reform, Karl vom Stein and Karl von Hardenberg, was to rejuvenate the humbled state and to stir up public support by granting as much civil liberty to the individual subject as they thought safe, while keeping the power of the monarchy and bureaucracy intact. In September 1807, as the streets of Berlin rang to the sound of French boots, Hardenberg declared from Riga that the reforms would be 'a revolution in a positive sense...to be made not through violent impulses from below or outside, but through the wisdom of the government'.

Stein and Hardenberg accepted that some public participation in government was needed in order to secure support for the reforms and the monarchy. Both talked about introducing a constitution because, Stein wrote in June 1807, 'the nation, despite all its flaws, possesses a noble energy, valour, and willingness to sacrifice itself for fatherland and freedom'. Yet for King Frederick William III a constitution was a step too far and was not introduced. The other reforms were nonetheless momentous: the October Edict of 1807 declared that from November 1810, serfdom would be abolished. All restrictions on landownership were removed, local government reformed, Jews given more civil rights, the power of the guilds reduced, and the tax system overhauled. The army reforms fell short of Gerhard von Scharnhorst's vision for a *Volksarmee*, a people's army modelled on the French nation-in-arms, which was too much for Frederick William.

Conscription remained based on a system first introduced in 1714: all able-bodied men aged between 18 and 40 were to register for conscription, and the kingdom was divided up into 'cantons', each with their own regiment. When volunteers alone fell short of the recruits needed, the enrolled civilians could be drafted. In peacetime, conscripts were released after their basic training, but put on reserve lists which could be called upon on the outbreak of war. By 1799, the canton system gave Prussia a pool of 2 million men who could be mobilized. There were changes aimed at turning the Prussian soldier into a 'citizen' rather than the passive tool of his officers. Flogging was curtailed and some French practices, including the corps system and the *ordre mixte*, were cherry-picked. The restrictions imposed on the size of Prussia's army (42,000 men) at Tilsit were circumvented by the *Krümper* system, whereby conscripts were trained and then put in the reserves, while the *Landwehr* law created a national militia. Altogether, the Prussians managed to bring 280,000 troops to bear against Napoleon at the Battle of Leipzig in 1813.

The reformers aimed at arousing a *Prussian* nationalism, but it was often expressed in wider German terms. The Prussian poet Heinrich von Kleist fantasized about an all-German uprising, after which French bones, picked bare by scavengers, would whiten the landscape (see Figure 11). In Berlin, Friedrich Jahn established a gymnastic movement, whose members were to be fit and supple, while also egalitarian, freedom-loving, and nationalist, becoming the ideal citizen-soldier. Egalitarian German nationalism pure and simple resonated with young romantics at the universities, but did not strike much of a chord elsewhere. When the 'War of Liberation' came in 1813, most Germans, and indeed Prussians, were moved more by older forms of patriotism, focused on the individual dynasty or state (*Staatspatriotismus*), or even a particular region (*Landespatriotismus*). Yet these traditional loyalties did not preclude the emergence of German nationalism. The Prussians appealed to areas of Germany which had never been Prussian

11. In this British version of a contemporary German caricature, Napoleon's face is made up of corpses, his trademark hat a death-bearing raven, his decoration a spider, and his coat a map of Germany marking the sites of his defeats, including Leipzig

territory, so calls for resistance to Napoleon could not invoke only Prussian patriotism. Instead, they evoked a language of *German* liberation, one which often harked back to the days of the historic Holy Roman Empire. How this language was used in different states still depended upon local concerns and loyalties, including the defence of religion (Catholic or Protestant) and the promise of restoration for those small states that had been 'mediatized'. Yet such local and traditional loyalties were increasingly expressed in German terms and so gave German nationalism a stronger appeal.

Not all Prussians responded enthusiastically to government exhortations in the war of 1813: with the creation of the *Landwehr*, many peasants in the east fled into Russian-occupied Poland rather than be drafted. Yet amongst the literate, urban young there was a genuine surge of patriotism. While the peasantry made up 75 per cent of the population and contributed 18 per cent of volunteers for the army, young men with a high-school or university education living in towns, who accounted for 2 per cent of the population, contributed 12 per cent of the volunteers. Most impressively of all, urban artisans constituted 7 per cent of the population, but 41 per cent of the volunteers. Conspicuous by their contribution within these groups were the recently emancipated Jews. Prussian patriotism was therefore an urban phenomenon and one in which women were mobilized, too. Women in the royal family created a 'Women's Association for the Good of Fatherland' to rouse women to donate money, jewellery, and their time to the war effort and by the war's end the organization had some 600 branches.

Prussia's 'unshackling' (as the process of reform was sometimes called) was not replicated on anywhere near the same scale among the other major old regime powers. It was not for lack of ideas or effort, but almost all the great coalition states had internal, structural problems which obstructed or discouraged a Prussian-style overhaul. Amongst those who faced the greatest challenges in this respect was Austria. The Austrians did attempt some important changes, particularly in the anti-French resurgence before Wagram. There were appeals to German patriotism on the eve of that disaster. One Habsburg proclamation declared that 'Our cause is the cause of Germany' and the monarchy might have harnessed an evolving German patriotism amongst its German-speaking subjects: in the Tyrol, the mobilization produced religious fervour—the number of reported miracles (sightings of the Virgin Mary and the saints, for example) shot up—but it also evoked some powerful expressions of political loyalties: as one peasant fighter put it, he wanted to 'fight for God; for the emperor; for religion and Fatherland'. While a far cry from the democratic, rights-based nationalism of the French, the appeal of country, monarch, and faith was still a potent triad of values.

In one respect, the Austrians streaked ahead of the Prussians, forming a *Landwehr* as early as 1808. Soldiers were to be flogged less, an attempt was made to modernize the artillery and to train some light infantry battalions. A new civil code was introduced in 1811. Yet even the leading military reformer in Vienna, Archduke Charles, would only dip his toe in the water: the elites across the multi-ethnic empire were sensitive to any hint of a frontal assault on their privileges. Many towns and provinces were historically exempt from conscription: the Tyrol and the Croatian 'Military Frontier' because they provided irregular militias instead, while troop levies in Hungary needed the approval of the habitually fractious Hungarian Diet. Hungary was not allowed a *Landwehr*, since it might just as easily be deployed against the Habsburgs as against Napoleon. When the Diet obstructed financial reform in 1812, it was dismissed by a furious Emperor Francis. The monarchy remained heavily in debt and the economy impoverished by the runaway inflation of the paper currency introduced during the war, the *Bankozettel*. Once confronted with the actual possibility of combat in 1809, the first *Landwehr* battalions lost as much as 75 per cent of their ranks through desertion. It was all the more remarkable, therefore, that the Austrians were able to maintain an army of up to 425,000 troops at its peak, but they were raised in the traditional ways, through conscription with the normal raft of exemptions and buy-outs, although Charles reduced the term of service from fourteen to ten years in an attempt to soothe popular hostility.

Russia

While the Austrian government faced structural challenges in mobilizing its people for a national struggle, the Russian Empire faced two enormous obstacles: first, its vast geographical expanse. Communications were slow, roads often impassable, and state officials spread very thinly. The Tsar therefore leaned heavily on the nobility to levy taxes and raise recruits from their serfs. Serfdom was the second problem, since any major reform meant addressing this thorny issue. Tsar Alexander I toyed with the idea of turning his empire into a constitutional monarchy and liberating the serfs. This was driven less by hostility to France (he actually admired Napoleon), than by his own benign, vaguely liberal principles. He appointed an 'Unofficial Committee', which included such progressive minds as Mikhail Speransky, who by 1803 sadly concluded that Alexander was caught in a vicious circle: if the Tsar emancipated the serfs, he would alienate the nobility, whose prosperity was based heavily upon serfdom and upon whose cooperation the regime depended. On the other hand, if he granted a constitution without first freeing and then educating the peasantry, any legislature would be dominated by the nobles who could then block emancipation. There was, therefore, no overhaul of Russian society, but this made the mobilization of Russian resources all the more impressive.

In the Napoleonic Wars, one million men were conscripted, although since most of these were serfs, they hardly constituted a citizen-army. Crucially, the Russian steppes thundered with large herds of hardy and speedy horses, providing the empire with the largest reserve of cavalry mounts in the world. Less successful was the production of arms and munitions: Russia desperately lacked its own supplies of saltpetre and lead for ordnance, so was dependent upon imports. The empire was the world's leading producer of iron and had an expansive reserve of timber, but the armaments factories at Tula, St Petersburg, and beyond the Urals were never able to produce the numbers of muskets needed by the army, nor to match the quality of those produced in the west. It was perhaps for this reason that Russian tactics involved far denser formations of infantry and attack with the bayonet, supported by concentrations of artillery higher than any other army, in order to compensate for the inaccuracy of Russian firearms. Russian artillery underwent some dramatic changes, driven through by General Aleksei Arakcheev, inspector-general of artillery from 1803, so that by 1805, the quality and mobility of Russian guns matched those of any other army: by 1812, Russia may have had the best horse artillery in the Europe.

Arakcheev may have been, by all accounts, a difficult, tyrannical, and charmless character, but when he was Minister of War between 1808 and 1810 he made some improvements in the treatment of the hapless peasant conscripts. From 1808, they were accommodated in Reserve Recruit Depots, where discipline was milder than in the regiments and where dedicated instructors spent a good nine months in training the soldiers. The commanders of individual regiments also sought to reduce flogging and to treat their serf conscripts with more humanity.

In the context of serfdom, there could be little talk of a 'people's war' against Napoleon. Rather, the Russians were told that they were fighting for God and the Tsar. In March 1812, Speranksy was dismissed as Alexander I's state secretary and replaced by the conservative thinker Admiral Alexander Shishkov, who drafted patriotic proclamations exhorting all Russians to rise in defence of the Tsar, Fatherland, and Orthodoxy. The governor of Moscow, another conservative patriot, Count Fedor Rostopchin (who later was credited, if that is the word, with burning down his own city), issued bulletins in which he appealed to the people's visceral instincts, urging them resist the foreign invaders. Orthodox priests told peasants that Napoleon was the representative of the Antichrist. One Russian newspaper did envisage a mass uprising against the French, in which 'the peasants, armed with peasant axes, scythes, pitchforks and spears fight with them and fall upon them, then the French are vanquished and our brave peasants beat them roundly, in the defence of faith and the fatherland'. Yet this was precisely what the elites feared most, since they knew that, unless they channelled the patriotic energy of the masses, there was every chance that they, and not the French, could become its victims. Memories were still raw of the last great peasant insurrection, the uprising led by Emelian Pugachev in 1773, in which the government lost control of large areas of Russia, manor houses were torched, and nobles and their families butchered. As war with France approached, there was genuine apprehension that Napoleon would issue a proclamation emancipating the serfs and so provoke another uprising.

Yet in the event, Russian popular resistance was aimed against Napoleon, although the motivations of the peasants are hard to discern with any great certainty. There is evidence that they were driven by devotion to the Orthodox faith: one peasant who enlisted his three sons declared of the invaders that 'We shall not let the miscreants drink our Orthodox blood.' Soviet historians emphasized the patriotic mobilization of the people in partisan warfare. The term *partizan* was certainly used by the Russians in 1812, but it meant the use of small detachments of regular light cavalry and Cossacks against French stragglers: peasants assisted in providing intelligence and as guides, but they did not form the core of the units. They did serve in the militia, but they could not volunteer, since they were 'owned' by their landlords, who decided who would be enrolled. The militia, which was established as an emergency measure in July 1812, eventually drew in some 230,000 men for the duration of the campaign. Where active peasant resistance did take place was in the regions closest to Napoleon's line of advance in the summer of 1812: they were provoked by marauding French foraging parties who plundered food and fodder for their horses. Marshal Kutuzov told the Tsar that the peasants hid their families in the forests before returning to defend their villages against the French. Moreover, 'quite often even the women' helped to trap and kill the enemy.

Britain

Paradoxical though it may sound, the British government faced a different challenge in mobilizing its people: namely, it was acutely aware of its own 'liberties'. The British public was hostile to the notion of conscription and a standing army, both of which may have sat well with a tyrannical ogre like Bonaparte, but were an affront to the liberties of freeborn Britons. Commanders certainly wanted some form of compulsory service, but the most they got was an expansion of the militia, recruited by a conscription ballot but intended only for home service. They could only hope that militia service would give some men enough of a taste for the military life that they would volunteer for the regulars: 146,000 men did so between 1793 and 1815. There was also a programme of reforms led by the Duke of York from 1804 aimed at making service more attractive by improving the ordinary soldier's well-being, but also fostering a sense of professionalism. Soldiers were to be separated from civilian life and motivated by regimental pride. This was quite the opposite of the French ideal of the 'nation-in-arms': officers told their men to 'look to their corps as their country, and to their officer as their only protector'. Catholic soldiers were given more religious freedom (of great import in an army which recruited a lot of Irishmen); and veterans were promised pensions.

Yet British generals grumbled that voluntary service alone could never satiate the army's appetite for cannon-fodder. Regiments resorted to ugly methods of recruitment: thugs called 'crimps' trawled the streets and ale-houses for victims to press-gang, individual militiamen were bullied into 'volunteering', while in Scotland, lairds ruthlessly exploited the tenant–landlord relationship to pressurize Highlanders into service. At its peak, in 1813, the British army boasted 330,000 men, but the combat-effective regulars had to be split between the colonies, garrison duties in the British Isles, and fighting on the Iberian Peninsula, where Wellington was never given more than 60,000 troops. Yet the British army made up for its (relatively) diminutive size by its effectiveness: few other armies could claim to be able to deploy their battalions in thin lines, two ranks deep, and be able to stop the onrushing French columns with the accuracy of its musket-fire. In any case, the figures for the British army overlook the importance of Britain's naval strength and the East India Company's forces in India, mostly made up of Indian troops, which an 1815 estimate brought the total British military strength to just over one million, putting it on a par with the other great European powers.

Just as French soldiers wrote home to express their feelings about the conflict, so too did their British counterparts. After fighting along the northern French frontier in 1793, a Scottish corporal wrote to his mother that he wanted to 'do more yet for my King & Country's saik'. It has been estimated that if 10 per cent of the adult male population joined the regulars in the period between 1793 and 1815, that proportion rises to a sixth if the volunteers and the militia are taken into account. Enthusiasm fluctuated: there were usually rushes to the colours in times of invasion scare (in 1798 and around 1803), followed by a dip after 1804, then another surge with the news of the Spanish uprising in 1808, which was reported widely in the British press and followed with keen interest by the public.

The British government could by and large rely on the support of the population for the war effort. Such support was never consistent (and indeed could be highly volatile and dependent as much on material concerns and local politics as on patriotism), but it was always present. A patriotism evolved which may have been more explicitly 'British'—in a sense, this was necessary, given that a third of officers and men in the army were Irish and, respectively, a quarter and a sixth were Scottish. But there were also values that cemented public loyalties, such as the monarchy, the 'ancient constitution', the empire and its spoils, as well as old-fashioned Francophobia. Women, usually but not exclusively middle-class, mobilized their energies and organizational capabilities to provide clothing for the troops and collect funds for the war effort, for the wounded and the widowed. Hundreds of subscription lists survive in which women's names appear—often in their hundreds. Meanwhile, there was a resurgence of British radicalism towards the end of the war, demanding political rights and the reform of a parliament based on a very limited suffrage. While this might seem to contradict a public patriotism devoted to the existing order, it was actually a direct product of it: British men and women alike, in mobilizing for the war against France, claimed a stake in the civic order and, by extension, demanded the rights of citizenship.

Important though the British campaigns on land and sea were, they were accompanied by a contribution to the war which proved to be of equal, if not greater, significance: money. With their small army and their maritime commitments, the British were well aware that they could not win without the help of continental allies who could match French manpower. Parsimoniously at first, the British encouraged their allies to mobilize by subsidizing their war efforts. Some politicians were queasy about this, since it looked as though the British were paying Europeans to fight their battles for them: as one Member of Parliament complained in 1800, 'even our allies had said that the English covered Germany with blood and gold'. Yet the British financial commitment mushroomed and played a critical role in the final push against Napoleon's empire: of the £65.83 million sent to Britain's allies almost half was paid out in 1813–15. While a long way from covering the military expenses of the coalition, the money helped to keep its armies in the field after the exhaustion of years of war, exploitation, and defeat.

The British were able to do this for two reasons. First, over the course of the eighteenth century, Britain had almost developed into the prototype of the 'fiscal-military state', the salient features of which were an efficient, centralized revenue system able to sustain armed forces. Secondly, the British government was able to maintain its credit on the international money markets and so borrow deeply in order to fund its war effort. Britain was not a democracy, but it had a parliament which limited the power of the government. Yet rather than hamper the state's efforts to pursue foreign policy, the parliamentary system actually strengthened it, for though it represented the interests of the landed elites, their own financial interests were bound up with commerce and the proceeds of empire, so that, on this issue at least, they often found common ground with the government.

The result was that the government could raise taxation, borrow money, and spend it on the war with little opposition from among the elites, although such measures as the 'income tax' introduced in 1799 were certainly unpopular. Moreover, the British could tap the resources of their manufacturing and commerce. Yields from taxes on consumption had grown in the eighteenth century because of domestic economic growth, including the incipient expansion in manufacturing which would later take off in full-blown industrialization. The lead that British manufacturing already had over its European competitors was certainly an advantage in the conflict, not least because the largest single consumer of manufactured products in the world at the time was probably the Royal Navy.

In addition, there were the spoils of empire: 7 per cent of government revenue came from the duties imposed on tea, while imports of West Indian sugar paid duty worth 50 per cent of its value by 1815. The state also creamed off money from British commerce in India, raising £5 million annually. A combination of the political consent of the elites and the proceeds from manufacturing and commerce usually reassured the government's lenders that the debts would be honoured, a confidence which allowed Britain's national debt to rise from £245 million in 1793 to £834 million by war's end. It also ensured that Napoleon's calculation that the continental blockade would destroy British finances would never quite come true (although they came to the brink in the downturn of 1811). The importance of commerce to the vigour of the British war effort was one reason why the government always gave special attention to the needs of the Royal Navy.

Overall, the extent to which Europeans were mobilized by ideological commitment to nationalism or to more traditional values is very patchy and, in any case, the two often overlapped. Yet, as this and preceding chapters have shown, the conflict did absorb the active participation of a swathe of the population in a multitude of ways, voluntarily or otherwise, and to wildly different degrees of enthusiasm. Even if the conflict was not a clash of nationalisms, the very intensity of the struggle, and the ways in which it touched the lives of millions, definitely made the conflict a 'people's war'.

Conclusion: legacies

It is fashionable today to magnify Bonaparte's victories:
those who suffered by them disappeared; we no longer hear
the curses of the victims and their cries of pain and distress;
we no longer see France exhausted, with only women to till
her soil … we no longer see the conscription notices pasted
up at street corners, and the passers-by gathering in a crowd
in front of those huge lists of the dead, looking in
consternation for the names of their children, their brothers,
their friends, their neighbours.

François-René de Chateaubriand committed these dark thoughts
to his memoirs, which he completed in 1839. As a French
royalist, he could be expected to be hostile to Napoleon and to
his legacy, but he nonetheless captured the widespread human
suffering inflicted by the war. As both a diplomat and a writer,
Chateaubriand was frustrated but not surprised by the apparent
ease with which his compatriots seemed to have forgotten,
within a generation, the devastation and remembered only
the glories.

Napoleon himself was partly responsible for this. Entrapped on
St Helena from 1815 until his death in 1821, he spoke at great
length with his secretary, Emmanuel de Las Cases, who recorded

his Emperor's ruminations in detail. Las Cases's book, *Mémorial de Saint-Hélène,* was published shortly after Napoleon's death and it became the most successful Napoleonic memoir ever written, partly because it brought together and articulated in one work the elements of the myth already circulating amongst the French public—the victories, the Empire, the saviour of the Revolution—but also because, for the first time since Waterloo, Napoleon once more had a voice. That voice uttered inspirational words which found a sympathetic ear amongst French liberals who, in the 1820s, were engaged in their own political struggle against royalists and reactionaries. The name of Napoleon meant not only military glory, but also the defence and spread of the emancipating ideals of the French Revolution.

As with many myths, there is a germ of truth buried beneath them. Napoleon may have been trying to delude himself and posterity, but there were elements in his Empire which did bring about positive changes: he was not Hitler, with whom he is often compared. The Napoleonic Code guaranteed civil equality wherever it was introduced and it attacked privilege, although here its record is patchier, particularly in its abolition of the rights of lords over their peasants. The same Code offered Napoleon's subjects a legal system which was generally fair, cheap, accessible, and incorrupt. Where the Concordat was applied in the Empire, it emancipated religious minorities, particularly Jews, sometimes over the violent opposition of the masses whose prejudices were deeply entrenched. The Napoleonic gendarmerie proved to be remarkably successful in bringing law and order to the borderlands traditionally riven with banditry. For European liberals in the generation or so after 1815, as well as for many historians since, these were positive achievements which—up to a point—compensated for the devastation and suffering of the wars. When the Prussians annexed the Rhineland in 1815, the German population there successfully insisted that the Code be kept—and it was until the end of the century. Even where the returning monarchies tried to sweep away all traces of the Napoleonic order, once the dust had settled, many of the changes were quietly reintroduced. In Piedmont in Italy, the gendarmerie was too useful to be abolished: renamed the *Carabinieri*, they formed the basis of its modern Italian equivalent. Elements of the Napoleonic Code were also brought back after a few years. In Rome, governed once again by the Pope, religious zealots initially went so far as to ban vaccination and street lighting because they had been introduced by Napoleon, but fortunately cooler heads soon prevailed and some of the more constructive elements in the French legacy were restored.

Less convincing is the notion of Napoleon as the herald of European integration. When the French President Georges Pompidou led the bicentenary of Napoleon's birth in 1969, he stressed the Emperor's construction of a unified Europe, a myth that still has surprising resilience. The Continental System, the Code, the Concordat, and French administration certainly gave Europe a certain uniformity, but the first was aimed at economically benefiting France above all (as Napoleon himself admitted), while the fourth made the state more effective in raising recruits and money for the all-consuming furnace of the conflict.

The French Wars did, however, change the map of Europe irreversibly. As the revolutionary and Napoleonic juggernaut rolled across the continent, it crushed dozens of hapless states under its wheels. So, frankly, did the diplomatic responses of the allied powers as they sought to secure strategic advantage from the wars. In the processes of secularization and mediatization, as in Germany, or diplomatic wheeling-and-dealing, as in Italy, the diverse range of polities that had characterized the old regime disappeared. After 1815, city-states, sovereign fiefdoms, episcopal principalities (states ruled by bishops), and composite states made up of scattered territories that were not contiguous either disappeared or were severely reduced in number. The consolidated state became the rule.

The conservatives who tried to construct a stable post-war order from the debris at the Congress of Vienna in 1815 discovered that they neither would nor could reverse this state of affairs. Internationally, they had learned, through the very hard, repetitive knocks of the French Wars, that the old European system based on 'balance of power' politics could not restrain a powerful state with aggressive ambitions. The peace treaties that year therefore reordered Europe with the aim of reducing international friction, while satisfying, once and for all, some of the most pressing demands of the victors. To these ends, France was sealed in behind its frontiers of 1790, the Rhineland was annexed by Prussia, Italy cast under Austrian domination, and Belgium merged with the Netherlands into a united kingdom. In none of these cases did this involve a restoration of the old order.

In Italy, the arrangement confirmed what the French had already done: Genoa, annexed by Napoleon in 1805, remained part of the northern kingdom of Piedmont in order to buttress it against France. Venice, given to Austria by Bonaparte in 1797, was returned to Habsburg rule. In Germany, there was no going back to the 365 principalities, free cities, bishoprics, duchies, kingdoms, and knightly domains that had made the Holy Roman Empire the epitome of organic, old regime politics. The 18 states of Napoleon's Confederation of the Rhine were welded together with the remainder to create a 39-member German Confederation. The purpose was to ensure that Germany could protect itself from outside invasion with a federal army, while restraining the bitter contest between Austria and Prussia for dominance by guaranteeing the independence of Germany's smaller 'middle' states. The other source of eighteenth-century conflict was, it was hoped, dampened down: Poland was definitively carved up between Russia, Austria, and Prussia. So for all the talk by conservatives about restoring 'legitimate' regimes, the reality was that they were remarkably pragmatic to the point of accepting much of the recasting already left by the French Wars.

While aimed at ensuring a stable European order, these were not arrangements calculated to please Polish, Italian, or German nationalists who wanted unity and independence. If in 1815 most national movements were the preserve of elites, they did not remain so for long: the revolutions in 1830–3 and 1848–9 brought liberal nationalists onto the barricades across Europe. Napoleon had claimed credit as the emancipator of nations, telling de Las Cases that 'one of my greatest ideas was the agglomeration, the concentration of the same geographic peoples fragmented and dissolved by revolutions and politics'. Of the French, the Spanish, the Germans, and the Italians, he claimed, 'I wanted to turn each of those peoples into a single nationality' as the first step towards the creation of a 'great European family' of peoples united by enlightened ideals, similarities in laws, principles, and interests.

Certainly, Napoleon stimulated national feeling and perhaps nowhere more so than in Poland, which had loyally supported him to the very end, since he had restored something resembling Polish independence in 1807. Poland's stirring national anthem was originally called 'The Song of the Polish Legions in Italy': its author, Józef Wybicki, was amongst the exiles who had served within the army of Bonaparte's Cisalpine Republic in the late 1790s. Its lines evoke Napoleon: 'We've been shown by Bonaparte | Ways to victory.'

Napoleon was not averse to firing up the patriotism of his other European subjects when it suited him—the creation of the Napoleonic kingdom of Italy in 1805 fell far short of national unity, but it was partially aimed at raising hopes that the French represented the best chance for Italian independence and unification in the future. The Italian *tricolore* of red-white-green was first designed as the flag of the Cispadane Republic, created by Bonaparte in 1796. Napoleon's real motives, however, were military, for both Poles and Italians figured strongly amongst the ranks of the *Grande Armée*. His treatment of Germany shows that he had no desire, as he later claimed, to foster movements for national unification. Napoleon's satellites had to be manageable and efficient, but they would never be allowed to reach such strength that they could challenge French hegemony. Nonetheless, for those Europeans who fought in Napoleon's armies, the inheritance was a potent one. In France and Italy, respectively, the *Charbonnerie* and the *Carbonari* were liberal underground organizations conspiring against the conservative order: they filled their ranks with disaffected soldiers who had served Napoleon, and revolutions in Italy in 1820–1 and again in 1831–2 were led by such men. The Poles who led the insurrection against tsarist oppression in 1831 were, first and foremost, army officers, many of whom had been veterans of the *Grande Armée*.

Yet if the Napoleonic Wars stimulated a nationalist or liberal legacy, it was as much in opposition to the French imperium as in support of it. The resistance to Napoleon was rarely motivated by modern nationalism, but by more traditional loyalties, sometimes overlaid by nationalist language. Nonetheless, as the conflict receded into the past and as nationalism began to win more converts amongst the peoples of Europe, the Napoleonic Wars were increasingly commemorated as 'national' struggles for freedom. In Spain, the most potent symbol was that of the *guerrilla*, an icon adopted by both right and left. For conservatives, the 'War of Independence' was fought by the Spanish people who rejected the principles of the French Revolution in defence of the established order of Church and King. For the left, the *guerrillas* represented not only a struggle for national liberation, but also for revolution: 'The guerrillas were the nation in arms...They were both soldiers and citizens', wrote Rodriguez Solis, a republican historian who helped toppled Queen Isabella II in 1868 and create the First Spanish Republic in 1873. Marxists later saw the *guerrillas* as proto-revolutionaries, 'primitive rebels' against the social injustices of rural society.

In Germany, the campaigns of 1813–14 were remembered as the 'Wars of Liberation' and they left two weighty, symbolic legacies:

the Iron Cross and the German colours of black-red-gold. The Iron Cross was designed in 1813 to reward the courage of Prussian soldiers regardless of rank, while the Order of Luise (named for the King's beloved and departed wife) was awarded to women for contributions to the war effort. The black-red-gold colours of modern Germany stem from the uniforms of the Lützow Freikorps, a volunteer unit of the Prussian army, recruited in 1813 from university students and academics (who were clearly of a different fibre in those days). The black uniforms were given a dash of colour by the gold and red of the trim, the insignia, and flashes. The *Schwarz-rot-geld* was the banner of the liberals in the 1848 Revolutions, but there were other political legacies. The Nazis naturally exploited the imagery of the German 'War of Liberation' for their own ends: they were 'a symbol of the present...for the time of our own struggle', as the director of a propaganda film put it at the time. In 1953, which was not only the 150th anniversary of the 'War of Liberation', but also a year in which East German citizens protested and went on strike, demanding free elections, the Communist regime of the German Democratic Republic emphasized the role of Russo-German friendship in the victory, while recasting it as the triumph of the 'people' against monarchism and tyranny.

The Russians, too, experienced a complex legacy from the Napoleonic Wars. On the one hand, 1812 was the 'Patriotic War', an uprising of the whole Russian people against a foreign invader dwarfed only by the 'Great Patriotic War' of 1941–5. The parallels between popular resistance to Napoleon and the partisan fighters of the Second World War were too tempting for Soviet historians to ignore. On the other hand, the experience of Russian officers as they marched across Central Europe and into France planted the seed of liberal ideas. Entertained by German and even French officials, army officers, and nobles as they marched the length of Europe in 1812–14, they thought about the ways in which the reforms of the Napoleonic epoch might be applied successfully in Russia. After the war, frustrated by the Tsar's swing towards conservatism and religious mysticism, they formed societies aimed initially at educational and social reform, but which evolved into an underground revolutionary organization aimed against the entire tsarist system. In the epilogue of *War and Peace*, Tolstoy has the central characters, noblemen and veterans of the war, discussing the creation of a society to oppose the reactionaries, 'people who are strangling and destroying everything', and so he anticipates the liberal army officers who became the first Russian revolutionaries in 1825, the Decembrists, who tried in vain to topple Nicholas I as he became Tsar in the month which gave the insurgents their name.

Yet perhaps the weightiest legacy of the Napoleonic Wars is global rather than European. Here, ironically enough, Napoleon *was* a liberator, but only in an indirect and indeed unintentional way. When his invasion of Egypt in 1798 failed, the Turkish Sultan appointed a dynamic Albanian soldier, Muhammad Ali, as pasha, or governor, who modernized the country to such an extent that it became powerful enough to challenge its own Ottoman masters. The French assault also weakened the Sultan's grip on his Balkan provinces, provoking the Serbian revolution in 1804—the first but by no means the last struggle for independence from Turkish rule. Napoleon's attempts to restore slavery in the French Empire precipitated a struggle for freedom which culminated in the independence of Haiti, to this date the second longest-lived republic in the western hemisphere after the United States.

Napoleon's efforts to control Spain from 1808 broke the political bonds between Spain and its Latin American colonies, giving patriots there the chance to marshal their strength, hone their ideas, and then strike out for independence, a goal which was won across South and Central America after two decades of grinding, tortuous warfare—and here, too, Napoleonic veterans found plenty of opportunities to practise their bloody trade. The global repercussions of the conflict strengthened the British hold on

India, expanded their empire in Asia and the Caribbean, and left them as the pre-eminent imperial power in the world. So in their political legacies, in their mobilization of entire societies, and in their global reach, the French Wars of 1792–1815 presaged the total wars of the twentieth century. They accelerated the emergence of the world that we inhabit today.

References

Introduction

Paul Schroeder, *The Transformation of European Politics 1763–1848* (1994), 393.

Charles Esdaile, *Napoleon's Wars: An International History, 1803–1815* (2007), 12–13.

Chapter 1: Origins

Leo Tolstoy (trans. Anthony Briggs), *War and Peace* (2005), 908.

Abbé Raynal, *L'Abbé Raynal aux États-Généraux* (Marseille, 1789), 5.

Scots Magazine in Paul Dukes, *The Making of Russian Absolutism, 1613–1801* (1982), 175.

Frederick the Great in Christopher Clark, *The Iron Kingdom: The Rise and Downfall of Prussia 1600–1947* (2006), 216.

Petition from Pondichéry in Archives Nationales d'Outre-Mer (Aix-en-Provence), Archives de Pondichéry, vol. 50, fo. 51.

De Ségur in Tim Blanning, *The Origins of the French Revolutionary Wars* (1986), 51.

Declaration of Peace in Jacques Godechot, *La Grande Nation: L'expansion révolutionnaire de la France dans le monde de 1789 à 1799* (1983), 66.

Robespierre in Blanning, *Origins*, 113.

Chapter 2: The French Revolutionary Wars, 1792–1802

David Lloyd George, *War Memoirs, 1914–15* (1933), 49.

Bischoffwerder quoted in Tim Blanning, *The Pursuit of Glory: Europe 1648–1815* (2007), 666.

Danton in William Doyle, *Oxford History of the French Revolution* (1989), 201.

Goethe in David Bell, *The First Total War: Napoleon's Europe and the Birth of Warfare as we Know it* (2007), 131.

Danton in Godechot, *La Grande Nation*, 72.

Tim Blanning, *The French Revolutionary Wars, 1787–1802* (1996), 115.

British commander quoted in Blanning, *Pursuit of Glory*, 633.

Chapter 3: The Napoleonic Wars, 1803–1815

La Revellière-Lépeaux in Blanning, *Origins*, 178.

Richard Wellesley in Michael Edwardes, *Glorious Sahibs: The Romantic as Empire-Builder 1799–1838* (1968), 32.

Schroeder, *Transformation*, 228–9.

Belgrano quoted in R. A. Humphreys and John Lynch (eds.), *The Origins of the Latin American Revolutions 1808–1826* (1965), 280.

Esdaile, *Napoleon's Wars*, 396–9.

Russian aide in Dominic Lieven, *Russia against Napoleon: The Battle for Europe, 1807 to 1814* (2009), 131.

Chapter 4: Total war, revolutionary war

Levée en masse in Blanning, *French Revolutionary Wars*, 100–1.

Revolutonary (Dubois-Crancé) in *Archives parlementaires de 1787 à 1860: Recueil complet des débats législatifs et politiques des chambres françaises* 1ère série, 96 vols. (1877–1990), x. 520.

Carl von Clausewitz, *On War* (1968), 385.

French soldiers in Alan Forrest, *Napoleon's Men: The Soldiers of the Revolution and Empire* (2002), 87, 90.

Pierre Delaporte, 'Campagne de l'an II: Journal du Conscrit Pierre Delaporte', *Nouvelle Revue rétrospective* 11 (1899), 388–90.

Theobald Wolfe Tone, *Memoirs of Theobald Wolfe Tone*, 2 vols. (1827), ii. 11.

Napoleon and the *Courier of the Army of Italy* in Bell, *First Total War*, 197, 199.

Austerlitz veteran in Esdaile, *Napoleon's Wars*, 221.

Tsar Alexander in Lieven, *Russia against Napoleon*, 92.

Lucien Bonaparte in Martyn Lyons, *Napoleon Bonaparte and the Legacy of the French Revolution* (1994), 70.

Prefect in 1813 in Forrest, *Napoleon's Men* (2002), 10.

Napoleon in Lyons, *Napoleon Bonaparte*, 44.

American consul in François Crouzet, 'Wars, Blockade, and Economic Change in Europe, 1792–1815', *Journal of Economic History* 24 (1964), 571n.

Chapter 5: Soldiers and civilians

Vattel quoted in Bell, *First Total War*, 48, 51.

British adjutant-general in J. E. Cookson, *The British Armed Nation 1793–1815* (1997), 124.

British officer in Cookson, *British Armed Nation*, 121.

Barclay de Tolly in Lieven, *Russia against Napoleon*, 108–9.

Bavarian commander in Adam Zamoyski, *1812: Napoleon's Fatal March on Moscow* (2004), 191.

French cavalryman in Forrest, *Napoleon's Men*, 141.

French PoW in Forrest, *Napoleon's Men*, 158.

Jean-Roch Coignet, *Les Cahiers du Capitaine Coignet* (1883).

Wellington in Daniel Rignault and David Wherry, 'Lessons from the Past Worth Remembering: Larrey and Triage', *Trauma* (1999), 88.

The Memoirs of Sergeant Bourgogne 1812–1813 (1979), 66–7.

Scottish soldier in Richard Holmes, *Redcoat: The British Soldier in the Age of Horse and Musket* (2001), 366.

Napoleon's order in Lyons, *Napoleon Bonaparte*, 25.

French officer in Tim Blanning, *The French Revolution in Germany: Occupation and Resistance in the Rhineland, 1792–1802* (1983), 98.

British officer in Holmes, *Redcoat*, 391.

Leipzig journalist quoted in Karen Hagemann, '"Unimaginable Horror and Misery": The Battle of Leipzig in October 1813 in Civilian Experience and Perception', in Alan Forrest, Karen Hagemann, and Jane Rendall (eds.), *Soldiers, Citizens and Civilians: Experiences and Perceptions of the Revolutionary and Napoleonic Wars, 1790–1820* (2009), 166.

Chapter 6: The war at sea

Bonaparte in Blanning, *French Revolutionary Wars*, 196.

Wellington in Nicholas Rodger, *The Command of the Ocean: A Naval History of Britain, 1649–1815* (2004), 564.

Marsden in Rodger, *Command of the Ocean*, 482.

William Dillon, *A Narrative of my Personal Adventures (1790–1839)*, 2 vols. (1956), ii. 10–11.

A. Crawford, *Reminiscences of a Naval Officer: A Quarter-Deck View of the War against Napoleon* (1999), 11.

Nelson's orders in Julian Corbett, *The Campaign of Trafalgar*, 2 vols. (1919), ii. 496–9.

British sailor in Édouard Desbrière, *La Campagne maritime de 1805: Trafalgar* (1907), 135.

Spanish captain in John Harbron, *Trafalgar and the Spanish Navy* (1988), 102.

Naval combat in John Westwood, 'Witnesses of Trafalgar', in John Terraine, *Trafalgar* (1976), 189–90.

Chapter 7: The people's war

Clausewitz in Bell, *First Total War*, 10.

Gneisenau in Brendan Simms, *The Struggle for Mastery in Germany, 1779–1850* (1998), 75.

Fichte quoted in John Breuilly, 'The Response to Napoleon and German Nationalism', in Alan Forrest and Peter Wilson (eds.), *The Bee and the Eagle: Napoleonic France and the End of the Holy Roman Empire, 1806* (2009), 260.

Spanish constitution quoted in W. N. Hargreaves-Mawdsley (ed.), *Spain under the Bourbons, 1700–1833: A Collection of Documents* (1973), 238.

Michael Broers, *Napoleon's Other War: Bandits, Rebels and their Pursuers in the Age of Revolutions* (2010), 110–11.

Wellington in Charles Esdaile, *Fighting Napoleon: Guerrillas, Bandits and Adventurers in Spain, 1808–1814* (2004), 156.

John L. Tone, *The Fatal Knot: The Guerrilla War in Navarre and the Defeat of Napoleon in Spain* (1994).

Hardenberg in Matthew Levinger, *Enlightened Nationalism: The Transformation of Prussian Political Culture, 1806–1848* (2000), 46.

Stein in Matthew Levinger, 'The Prussian Reform Movement and Enlightened Nationalism' in Philip G. Dwyer (ed.), *The Rise of Prussia 1700–1830* (2000), 263–4.

Russian newspaper in Janet Hartley, 'Russia and Napoleon: State, Society and the Nation', in Michael Rowe (ed.), *Collaboration and Resistance in Napoleonic Europe: State-Formation in an Age of Upheaval, c.1800–1815* (2003), 192.

Russian peasant in Hartley, 'Russia and Napoleon', 190.

Kutuzov in Lieven, *Russia against Napoleon*, 219.

Scottish corporal in Emma Vincent Macleod, *A War of Ideas: British Attitudes to the Wars against Revolutionary France, 1792–1802* (1998), 183.

Member of Parliament in John Sherwig, *Guineas and Gunpowder: British Foreign Aid in the Wars with France, 1793–1815* (1969), xiv.

Conclusion: legacies

François-René de Chateaubriand, *Memoirs of Chateaubriand* (1965), 294.

Napoleon in Emmanuel de Las Cases, *Mémorial de Sainte-Hélène, ou journal où se trouve consigné, jour par jour, ce qu'a dit et fait Napoléon durant dix-huit mois*, 2 vols. (1840), ii. 336.

Nazi film director in Clark, *Iron Kingdom*, 661.

Leo Tolstoy, *War and Peace* (2005), 1304.

Further reading

The French Wars, and the Napoleonic Wars in particular, have been
well researched, but there are always new directions, new
controversies. The list that follows can only offer a tiny selection
of the most useful works, most of them representing the latest
research, and it focuses on those books which offer the bigger
picture—surveys, armed forces, the Napoleonic Empire, the
belligerents, the global impact, and the legacies. It does not offer any
biographies of commanders or accounts of individual battles
or campaigns (except where they are especially helpful in illuminating
the broader issues). Readers who want to follow up with such detail
will find plenty of suggestions in the bibliographies of the books listed
here. The list is also confined to works published in English. For
readers with other languages, there are even deeper seams of material
to be mined.

Broad surveys

David Bell, *The First Total War: Napoleon's Europe and the Birth of
   Warfare as we Know it* (2007). A fascinating if grim exploration of
   the French Wars as a total war.
Tim Blanning, *The French Revolutionary Wars, 1787–1802* (1996).
   Combines lively analysis with sparkling narrative.
—— *The Origins of the French Revolutionary Wars* (1986). A detailed,
   lively analysis of the causes of the wars, full of acute observations.
David Chandler, *The Campaigns of Napoleon* (1966). A classic military
   history.

Owen Connolly, *Blundering to Glory: Napoleon's Military Campaigns* (1987). Controversial for its assessment of Napoleon's motivations.

Charles Esdaile, *Napoleon's Wars: An International History, 1803–1815* (2007). Excellent.

—— *The Wars of Napoleon* (1995). Offers a useful country-by-country discussion.

David Gates, *The Napoleonic Wars 1803–1815* (1997). A fine analysis, easy to navigate.

Gunther Rothenberg, *The Art of Warfare in the Age of Napoleon* (1977). An essential analysis.

Paul Schroeder, *The Transformation of European Politics 1763–1848* (1994). An impressive history of international relations; unambiguously condemns Napoleon.

Armed forces

Roy and Lesley Adkins, *Jack Tar: The Extraordinary Lives of Ordinary Seamen in Nelson's Navy* (2008). A splendid study of life in Britain's 'wooden walls'.

Rafe Blaufarb, *The French Army, 1750–1820: Careers, Talent, Merit* (2002). A rich analysis.

William S. Cormack, *Revolution and Political Conflict in the French Navy, 1789–1794* (2002). A groundbreaking work.

Gordon Craig, *The Politics of the Prussian Army, 1640–1945* (1955). A classic account of the role of the military within the Prussian state.

George Daughan, *If by Sea: The Forging of the American Navy from the Revolution to the War of 1812* (2008). A fine account.

Alan Forrest, *Napoleon's Men: The Soldiers of the Revolution and Empire* (2002). Describes the lives of French soldiers with a penetrating use of the sources.

John Harbron, *Trafalgar and the Spanish Navy* (1988). A useful analysis of a subject still neglected by anglophone historians.

Richard Holmes, *Redcoat: The British Soldier in the Age of Horse and Musket* (2001). A fascinating account of life in the British army.

John A. Lynn, *The Bayonets of the Republic: Motivation and Tactics in the Army of Revolutionary France, 1791–94* (1984). A well-written analysis of the rank and file.

Nicholas Rodger, *The Command of the Ocean: A Naval History of Britain, 1649–1815* (2004). A deep, rich survey of the Royal Navy by its leading modern historian.

Peter Wilson, *German Armies: War and German Society, 1648–1806* (1998). An excellent analysis.

The French conquests and the Napoleonic empire: occupation, collaboration, and resistance

Tim Blanning, *The French Revolution in Germany: Occupation and Resistance in the Rhineland, 1792–1802* (1983). A thematic, lively, detailed analysis.

Michael Broers, *Europe under Napoleon 1799–1815* (1996). One of the best single-volume analyses of the Napoleonic impact.

—— *The Napoleonic Empire in Italy, 1796–1814: Cultural Imperialism in a European Context?* (2005). Superb and thought-provoking.

—— *Napoleon's Other War: Bandits, Rebels and their Pursuers in the Age of Revolutions* (2010). A rich, readable, penetrating, deeply researched book.

Owen Connolly, *Napoleon's Satellite Kingdoms* (1965). A helpful survey.

Philip Dwyer (ed.), *Napoleon and Europe* (2001). A fine, useful collection of essays.

Geoffrey Ellis, *The Napoleonic Empire* (1991). A useful introduction.

Charles J. Esdaile (ed.), *Popular Resistance in the French Wars: Patriots, Partisans and Land Pirates* (2005). A fascinating collection of essays.

Alexander Grab, *Napoleon and the Transformation of Europe* (2003). A handy country-by-country discussion.

Michael Rowe (ed.), *Collaboration and Resistance in Napoleonic Europe: State-Formation in an Age of Upheaval, c.1800–1815* (2003). Lively essays that nuance the image of 'conqueror versus conquered'.

Simon Schama, *Patriots and Liberators: Revolution in the Netherlands, 1780–1813* (1977). A deeply researched narrative.

Stuart Woolf, *Napoleon's Integration of Europe* (1991). An essential, thematic analysis of the Napoleonic Empire.

The main belligerents

Austria, Prussia, and Germany

Christopher Clark, *The Iron Kingdom: The Rise and Downfall of Prussia 1600–1947* (2006). Excellent readable survey of Prussian history, with three chapters on our period.

Alan Forrest and Peter Wilson (eds.), *The Bee and the Eagle: Napoleonic France and the End of the Holy Roman Empire, 1806* (2009). Essays on the collision between France and the German states.

Matthew Levinger, *Enlightened Nationalism: The Transformation of Prussian Political Culture, 1806–1848* (2000). Essential for the Prussian response to Napoleon.

C. A. Macartney, *The Habsburg Empire, 1790–1918* (1969). An indispensable classic.

Michael Rowe, *From Reich to State: The Rhineland in the Revolutionary Age, 1780–1830* (2003). Deeply researched sweep through a transformative period.

Brendan Simms, *The Struggle for Mastery in Germany, 1779–1850* (1998). A pithy survey stressing the importance of international relations.

Britain

J. E. Cookson, *The British Armed Nation 1793–1815* (1997). A detailed analysis of the British wartime mobilization.

Clive Emsley, *British Society and the French Wars, 1793–1815* (1979). The standard work.

Emma Vincent Macleod, *A War of Ideas: British Attitudes to the Wars against Revolutionary France, 1792–1802* (1998). A superb, deeply researched analysis.

John Sherwig, *Guineas and Gunpowder: British Foreign Aid in the Wars with France, 1793–1815* (1969). How Britain supported one coalition after another.

France

Louis Bergeron, *France under Napoleon* (1981). Dissects the anatomy of the regime.

William Doyle, *The Oxford History of the French Revolution* (1989). A dynamic narrative, with chapters on the international impact and wars.

Georges Lefebvre, *Napoleon*, 2 vols. (1969). Gives all the essential detail, with important sections on the war.

Martyn Lyons, *Napoleon Bonaparte and the Legacy of the French Revolution* (1994). An excellent introduction to Napoleonic France, with two chapters on the European impact.

Jean Tulard, *Napoleon: The Myth of the Saviour* (1984). Now a classic.

Russia

John LeDonne, *The Russian Empire and the World, 1700–1917: The Geopolitics of Expansion and Containment* (1997). An original study of Russian geopolitics.

Dominic Lieven, *Russia against Napoleon: The Battle for Europe 1807 to 1814* (2009). Rich, readable account that stresses Russia's contribution to the allied victory.

Adam Zamoyski, *1812: Napoleon's Fatal March on Moscow* (2004). A vivid, harrowing, account.

Spain and Portugal

Charles Esdaile, *Fighting Napoleon: Guerrillas, Bandits and Adventurers in Spain, 1808–1814* (2004). Deeply researched, myth-busting.

—— *The Peninsular War: A New History* (2002). The best single-volume history.

John L. Tone, *The Fatal Knot: The Guerrilla War in Navarre and the Defeat of Napoleon in Spain* (1994). A rich, well-researched analysis.

The global impact

Michael S. Anderson, *The Eastern Question 1774–1923: A Study in International Relations* (1966). A now standard work on the diplomatic and strategic problems of the decline of the Ottoman Empire.

Jeremy Black, *The War of 1812 in the Age of Napoleon* (2009). Sets the American conflict in the global context of the Napoleonic Wars.

Juan Cole, *Napoleon's Egypt: Invading the Middle East* (2007). A cautionary tale with modern parallels.

George Daughan, *1812: The Navy's War* (2011). A lively naval history of the British–American conflict.

Jorge Domínguez, *Insurrection or Loyalty: The Breakdown of the Spanish American Empire* (1980).

Laurent Dubois, *Avengers of the New World: The Story of the Haitian Revolution* (2005). The most accessible account.

Michael Edwardes, *Glorious Sahibs: The Romantic as Empire-Builder 1799–1838* (1968). A lively history of British expansion in India.

Caroline Finkel, *Osman's Dream: The Story of the Ottoman Empire 1300–1923* (2005). A readable narrative with trenchant, wide-ranging chapters on our period.

Reginald Horsman, *The Causes of the War of 1812* (1962). A discussion of the British–American slide to war.

R. A. Humphreys and John Lynch (eds.), *The Origins of the Latin American Revolutions 1808–1826* (1965). A useful collection of documents.

Jon Latimer, *1812: War with America* (2007). Excellent.

John Lynch, *The Spanish-American Revolutions, 1808–1826* (1973). Still the standard account.

Jeremy Popkin, *You are All Free: The Haitian Revolution and the Abolition of Slavery* (2010). Tells the story of the war in Haiti until emancipation in 1794.

S. P. Sen, *The French in India 1763–1816* (1971). An indispensable, detailed guide.

Paul Strathern, *Napoleon in Egypt: 'The Greatest Glory'* (2008). A page-turner.

Jac Weller, *Wellington in India* (1972).

Gordon S. Wood, *Empire of Liberty: A History of the Early Republic, 1789–1815* (2009). A detailed, enjoyable assessment of the United States.

Legacies

Alan Forrest, *The Legacy of the French Revolutionary Wars: The Nation-in-Arms in French Republican Memory* (2009). The first major examination of the long-term impact of the mobilization of 1793.

Sudhir Hazareesingh, *The Legend of Napoleon* (2004). A textured, readable discussion of the myth in the nineteenth century.

Adam Zamoyski, *The Rites of Peace: The Fall of Napoleon and the Congress of Vienna* (2008). An excellent account, to be read alongside Schroeder (above).

Index

Index

Index

Expand your collection of
VERY SHORT INTRODUCTIONS